The Judas Church

An Obsession with Sex

— KEVIN CAREY —

Sacristy
Press

Sacristy Press
PO Box 612, Durham, DH1 9HT

www.sacristy.co.uk

First published in 2014 by Sacristy Press, Durham

Sacristy Limited, registered in England & Wales, number 7565667

British Library Cataloguing-in-Publication Data
A catalogue record for the book is available from the British Library

ISBN 978-1-908381-78-1

ACKNOWLEDGEMENTS

I wish to thank Hazel Ormond for her painstaking work on the text of this book, and particularly the tables; any errors are my own.

Kevin Carey
Hurstpierpoint
The Feast of Saint Peter and Saint Paul, 2014

CONTENTS

INTRODUCTION

If you ask most non-Christians in the United Kingdom to describe the core concern of Christianity they will most likely settle on ethics in general, and sexual ethics and gender roles in particular. In the course of writing this book I came across the following in a *Guardian* editorial on the eve of the November 2013 General Synod debate on women bishops which, I think, fairly expresses the general view:

> No-one much cares what the Church of England says about sex. That includes most church-goers. But those who play a part in deciding its line on such things mind more than enough to make up for the rest . . . Unblocking the stalled process of making women bishops matters but it is nothing like as important as the voice the Archbishop (Welby) has given the Church in the lives of the most vulnerable . . . As a double act with Pope Francis whose conspicuous humility and willingness to challenge the established orthodoxy in the Church of Rome is beginning to have a global impact, Dr. Welby is leading organised religion in this country into the kind of revival that seemed unimaginable a year ago. The deeper question is whether the Church of England wants to be in that place enough to put aside its obsession with sex. At the moment, it seems at least as likely that the Church will simply turn to the next doctrinal dispute and resume the course of irrelevance. The next last ditches that beckon are the celebration of gay marriage and the possibility of gay bishops. These are issues that those who are dedicated to upholding orthodoxy will find at least as absorbing as the last one.[1]

---

[1]   "Church of England: Mission Impossible", *The Guardian*, 19 November 2013.

That the Church of England should have spent so much energy on two matters of relative unimportance is bad enough. That this should have happened during the sharpest economic down-turn since the early 1930s, with its disproportionate consequences for the most disadvantaged, is nothing short of scandalous.

During the history of Christianity, certain issues have frequently assumed proportions far greater than the Bible would seem to admit—notably a persistently exaggerated emphasis on the role of the Virgin Mary before the Reformation, and an obsession with the mechanics of atonement and personal salvation after it. One would feel entitled to expect those who style themselves as 'Evangelicals' and who have inherited the tradition, if not always the practice, of *sola scriptura* to express their concerns broadly in line with scripture. However, I have long suspected that all is not well in this regard, starting with the admittedly unscientific perception that divorce and re-marriage are no less prevalent in Evangelical circles than in more 'liberal' sectors of Western Christianity. Or, to put it another way, it would be fair to argue that the Roman Catholic Church, which is farthest away in sentiment from *sola scriptura*, has been by far the most faithful and stringent upholder of what the Bible says about marriage or, at least, what Jesus says about it.

Why have some strands of Western Christianity been so ready to abandon the notion that marriage is a lifelong commitment of one man to one woman and to forbid sexual intercourse outside marriage, while so vehemently opposing the validity of same sex lifelong homosexual relationships? And what does it mean for a Church to oppose sex outside marriage when it welcomes couples to the nuptial altar accompanied by offspring from their current or previous non-marital relationships? These are critical issues in this book because the vast majority of Biblical references to sexual relationships emphatically forbid adultery which, as strictly interpreted, means any sexual relationship that a person has outside their marriage before or after divorce. I am not arguing on the one hand that adultery should be condoned nor on the other that people should not be allowed to divorce and re-marry. I am simply offering for consideration the questions of consistency and proportionality.

Regular reading of the Bible has subsequently prompted me to further thoughts which form the basis of this book. First, contrary to what most Christians and non-Christians alike believe to be the case, the amount of space in the Bible devoted to various aspects of the Second Commandment, that we should love our neighbour as ourself, is minute in comparison with the space devoted to the First, that we should love God above all things. In fact—and I mean "fact"—not only does the Bible have nothing to say about many of the ethical issues which concern us today, it says very little about the ethics of the times of its own authors. With the exception of the letters attributed to Saint Paul, The Book of Deuteronomy, and parts of the Books of Proverbs and Ecclesiasticus, there are no instances where it can be plausibly argued that ethical considerations have even approximate parity with the relationship between God and humans created in 'his' likeness.

Over time, I have further come to suspect that where the Bible speaks of ethics it is more concerned with power, wealth, and social and procedural justice than it is with sexual ethics. A good example of this is the strong priority of the dynastic over the ethical in the Book of Genesis. It is the primary purpose of this book to explore this particular thesis.

It is important at the outset to establish a fair concept of proportionality. It has long been held that respect for the Bible as the Word of God is indivisible, one pronouncement not being set in opposition to another, but I believe that it is fair to assert that we need to observe some proportionality in our reception. The obvious example is Biblical comment on homosexuality, where there are eight references, compared with scores on sexual conduct in general, primarily concerned with upholding marriage and condemning adultery, and even more concerning social justice. I think it is quite proper to say that the Bible is much more concerned with social justice than it is with homosexuality. By extension, I think it is fair to say that, on that basis, the Christian Church should reflect these concerns proportionately, and, furthermore, so should those who hold to the principle of *sola scriptura*. Conversely, this book will further argue that modern Christianity's disproportionate concentration on sexual and gender issues has seriously diverted it from its central purpose, proclaimed by Jesus, of establishing the Kingdom of Heaven on earth;, as Tom Wright would say, invoking the Lord's Prayer, "As it is in heaven".

During the protracted debates on the consecration of women bishops which I attended between 2005–10, proponents of women bishops were frequently accused of advocating their policy "simply on grounds of social justice and equality"; a strange accusation in view of the evidence of the Gospels. Jesus was unequivocally emphatic about social justice but said nothing either about the gender of his followers (although the 'discovery' of the Resurrection by women is surely iconic) or about a doctrine of a male monopoly of representation or presidency at meals commemorating the Last Supper.

Although I was brought up in the Roman Catholic Church, this is a quintessentially Protestant enterprise. During my theological studies I have picked up a smattering of New Testament Greek, particularly in connection with St Paul's Epistle to the Romans, but I am in no position to act as a referee concerning translations and I know no Hebrew at all. I must therefore fall back on the widely held view that the NRSV is the most reliable translation of the Bible from its various languages, and consequently I must study in the context of an act of trust; a stance which few 'Evangelicals', similarly handicapped, seem to recognise. A further complication is that the NRSV translators note a massive number of possible textual variants, and because I have chosen to read the NRSV text used in *The Jewish Annotated New Testament*, the text I use is not always the same as that customarily read in church. For these reasons, and many others, my analysis of the text will not always agree with other translations and there will be further room for disagreement over my analysis of the meaning of the text. In particular, I do not take "plain meaning" to be the same thing as literal reading. It is one of the great and peculiar paradoxes of our English-based culture to admire the literary merits of the Bible (particularly the

Authorised Version) while treating it like a chemistry text-book; a mistake already incipient at the Reformation and accentuated during the supposed Enlightenment. In this great library of diverse composition there must be a proper recognition of poetry, rhetoric, and analogy, and, for some interpretative traditions, there will also be room for symbolism, notably in reading the Old Testament as a foreshadowing of the New.

My calculations will therefore be approximate and the fact that they are neatly set out should not mislead readers into thinking that they are anything other than approximations. But if I am roughly correct in what I say, then Christians of all denominations should take notice.

I should say that, although I understand the argument of Scriptural indivisibility, I will develop in a later discussion the concept that, for the purposes of assigning importance to pronouncements, the teachings of Jesus should be ranked above the balance of the New Testament which should, in turn, be ranked above the Old Testament.

Having made my calculations as fairly as I can, I proceed to examine the recent Church of England pronouncements on sexual and gender issues. I do not think it unnecessary to provide any critical analysis of its pronouncements on social justice, which are unexceptionable, but which, I have learned from my grass roots experience, are much more greatly reverenced in the Parishes than they are at the General Synod. Indeed, a great deal of delay and near hysteria would have been avoided had such issues as the gender and sexuality of clergy been left to the House of Bishops.

Finally, I turn to what I believe is a betrayal of our Christian mission even greater than that of turning the multi-layered Biblical texts into monochrome moralism. Namely, the persistent obsession of Western Christianity with personal salvation rather than the building of God's Kingdom on earth. I will attempt to show that the political should take precedence over the social which should, in turn, take precedence over the individual. We have wrongly inverted this hierarchy so that we rank the personal as supreme, subordinating the social and leaving the political at the bottom of the ranking. The findings on the Biblical text are comforting in this respect but this case does not rely upon my earlier findings: it arises solely from what the Evangelists say Jesus cared about most, which is what we should care about most. However, we have tended to care much more about power, both political and personal. Our critics may have been, to say the least, ungenerous in pointing out Christian failings on social issues and in taunting us for our sexual obsessions, but their case is sound. We have allowed ourselves to fall into a 'liberal' trap by accepting that the Church of England must necessarily be home for any Christian who can recite the Creeds without thinking too much about them. Elizabeth I certainly never envisaged the inclusion of "Puritans" or "Roman Catholics" in the "Church by Law established", and although the Stuarts toyed with Roman Catholic entryism, this was an aberration in the first three centuries of the English Church. I shall never forget the grotesque experience at the General Synod of July 2010 while struggling for the enactment of legislation for the consecration of women bishops—long held to be both theologically and ecclesiologically coherent, and pastorally and missiologically desirable—of being heckled by priests, ordained only the week before, committed to reversing the ordination of women to their office. Just as the Militant Tendency almost destroyed the Labour Party, so these gender obsessed militants are undermining the credibility of the Church of England. Worse than that, they are impeding the mission of Jesus Christ. What counts is neither theological consistency, which is simply a correspondence of metaphors, nor the personal holiness of priests, although this is one of many necessary preconditions for a healthy Church. What counts, and what has always counted since the Resurrection, is the ability of Christ's gift, the Church, to be a proper channel for his message, particularly for those who need it most and, more often than not because they are the most difficult to reach, hear it least. It is to these people that this book is dedicated.

PART ONE: THE BIBLE

In the following exposition, citations are listed which deal with three broad clusters of issues:

- Sexuality and gender (S)
- Power and wealth (P)
- Procedural justice and mercy (J)

Each reference has an equal and unweighted score of one point. The first category (S) specifically refers to teaching about the role of women, the status of marriage, fornication, and adultery. The second (P) not only relates to teaching on power and wealth but, notably in the Letters (Section 2.3, p. 115), also refers to teaching on deprivation, suffering, endurance, and service, i.e., the advocacy of the loss or renunciation of wealth and power. Some may feel that P has too wide a scope to be fairly compared with S, but showing the two sides of wealth and power is the same as showing the two sides of faithful marriage. The third category (J) acts as a benchmark against which the scores of the other two can be judged. There is a particular problem with the concept of 'love' (see the introduction to Chapter 2, p. 85): I resisted the temptation to give it its own category (L), although my solution might slightly favour +S scores.

Each reference to one of these broad topics is noted to give an overall perspective on the salience of the issue in the context of the whole work. Where a reference is relevant to the subject matter of this book, the letter is preceded by a plus sign (+) and where I consider it not to be relevant it is preceded by a minus sign (-). It is important to remember that relevance to this book is a much narrower concept than relevance to the author and the intended audience, and so the scoring is not a judgment about the importance of the text in its initial milieu (cf. Isaiah 7.14). There are many marginal cases where it is not clear whether a reference is to one of the three broad topics, and there are also judgments to be made about analogy. This becomes particularly apparent in light of the depiction of idolatry as fornication or adultery; a particularly unfortunate use of words as it associates the denial of God in both the Old and New Testaments with an evil which is associated solely with women, not with male perpetrators. A sin that all commit would have been better.

Key references, such as those referring to homosexuality, are underlined. A citation may consist of part of a verse, a paragraph, or a whole chapter. Where two citations are identical, each is separately assigned, as I have adopted a charitable reading which credits authors with deliberate intention rather than accidental duplication.

I have resisted the obvious temptation to weight scores according to their origin. I personally hold that it is legitimate to rank, say, the sayings of Jesus over those of Paul where they disagree; and some might claim that the ethically-oriented Wisdom books should be weighted more favourably than accounts of monarchical behaviour in the Narratives. But in this Biblical survey I have treated all citations as of equal weight, regardless of context.

1.   THE OLD TESTAMENT

1.1.   THE PENTATEUCH (TORAH)

The first five books of the Old Testament, often referred to as the Pentateuch, are characterised in particular by the ubiquitous presence of God (YWHW) who is represented as speaking directly to the patriarchs and then to the legally foundational figure of Moses. The weight of the legal injunctions is derived directly from the performative speech acts in which God is said to be giving direct instructions. .

The issues of which we should take note in subsequent discussions are as follows:

- Whether Old Testament pronouncements on marriage are of any relevance to us today.
- To what extent does the Old Testament provide relevant ethical guidance on sexual matters?
- As the majority of Old Testament references relevant to our enquiry forbid adultery, how does this square with contemporary Christian attitudes to divorce?
- How well grounded are the texts on homosexuality as guidance for today?
- Why, if the account on the Old Testament of social justice and procedural justice is so overwhelming, do these subjects have less salience than sexual issues?

1.1.1.   Genesis

As the name implies, the main concern of the Book of Genesis is
about how things came to be and how they proceeded through the
generations, and so we would expect it to concentrate, as it does,
much more on sexual matters than social or procedural justice.
But, as we will see, it is not so unequivocally strait-laced as many
assume it to be. It introduces, without criticism, such concepts
as bigamy, concubinage, incest, and female gang rape to forestall
male gang rape.

1.26–28: +S
God creates man and woman, (apparently simultaneously) in 'his'
own image.

2.7: +S

2.21–25: +S
The sequential creation of the first man and then the first woman
in apparent contradiction to 1.26–28. This later account generates
a sequence of dependency which the earlier lacks. Perhaps because
the later account 'fits' better into the narrative in Chapters 2 and
3, or perhaps simply because it is more detailed and colourful, it
is the one which has been overwhelmingly accepted.

2.24: +S
This reference is widely accepted as God's sanction for monogamous
marriage, but there are some serious problems with this assertion.
First, it is Adam that is speaking in 2.24, not God. Secondly, as
we shall see, there was not an automatic acceptance in the Torah
of monogamous marriage, and it can be coherently argued that
Adam and Eve lived together and had sexual relations only with
each other because they had no choice as they were the only two
people in the narrative. Thirdly, it is at least plausible to argue that
the whole passage is an aetiology, an explanation of why things
are as they are, not an edict. Finally, and partly in opposition to

the previous point, this monogamous arrangement, if that is what it is, takes place before the Fall, or what we might call radically changed circumstances for human beings, which at least raises the question of whether we are expected to behave after the change in the same way in which Adam and Eve behaved before it. The pro-Fall argument places a strong and often exclusive emphasis on absolutely literal interpretation which, in this case, produces a serious contradiction as a literalist cannot allow the application of pre-Fall conditions to post-Fall conditions. This being so, the extension of the meaning of this verse to stipulate that all sexual relations must be monogamous is weak and the notion that this verse dictates monogamous, lifelong marriage, even weaker. Paradoxically, the less literally the passage is taken, the more powerful it is as an indicator of subsequent conduct, because, in the non-literalist interpretation, the conduct of the parties is more important than the legal framework in which they operate. In other words, faithfulness is more important than legislation.

2.25: -S
Adam and Eve are naked, often taken to be a sign of pre-Fall innocence, the corollary being post-Fall taboo.

3.6–7: -S
Eve eats of the tree of the knowledge of good and evil, but she can only have known of the injunction to desist from Adam as she had not been created when it was given in the second account of creation of which this is part (2.16–17). This is yet another incidence of disagreement between the two accounts, but the comment is legitimate within the second account. On that basis, the recipient of the direct command is surely more culpable than the indirect recipient. Furthermore, this is the first biblical example of the stereotype of the weak-willed female seductress whom the man cannot resist, a pathetic transference of responsibility. As it turns out, the couple did not die as God threatens in 2.17, which raises a whole host of problems of its own. I judge this reference

not to be relevant because it is the first of many which indulges in either ingrained or lazy misogyny which amounts to cliché.

3.16: +S

The critical reference for those who adopt a doctrine of ecclesiological 'male headship': " . . . your desire shall be for your husband, and he shall rule over you." Taken at face value, the severest interpretation of this reference is that within marriage the husband is in command of his wife, although it could be argued that this is an aetiology, a description of how things have come to be as they are. Nonetheless, there are no grounds whatsoever for extending this principle of matrimonial male hegemony to the sphere of public ecclesiastical life without adopting a strategy of interpretative extension, relying on a symbolic interpretation where this marriage represents the whole gender settlement for all time. The problem with this strategy is, yet again (cf. Genesis 2.24 above), that it cannot be selectively self-granted by 'literalists' to themselves but must be allowed to others. The alternative, to take the reference literally, is that it ties the interpreter to taking all statements literally, including those which are patently absurd or totally contradictory, cf. the death of Saul (1 Samuel 31.4; 2 Samuel 1.98–10).

4.19: -S

The first of many references to bigamy. I rule these out because it is not a burning issue for Christians today. However, it does call into question the 'hard' interpretation of 2.24.

9.22: -S

Ham is harshly punished for accidentally seeing his father, Noah, naked, cf. 2.25.

11.3: -S

Sarai is barren. The first of many references to this personal and sociological tragedy.

13.13: -S

The people of Sodom were sinners but their sin is not specified at this point and the inference that their only or chief sin is homosexuality (cf. 19.4–11) is not justified. What calls this most into question are later references to Sodom and Gomorrah which imply that the sin of the former city was idolatry, which is not unlikely in view of the analogy of sexual infractions being equated with idolatry (cf. Hosea 1–3, Ezekiel 22). Ezekiel 16.49 lists the sins of Sodom but, significantly, does not include the 'abomination' of homosexuality.

16.1–16: -S

Abraham fathers a child by Hagar with Sarai's consent. The first of many cases where conventional sexual mores are ranked second to dynastic continuity, a principle we would surely not extend to twenty-first century practice, which renders it irrelevant but which also further undermines the supposed Biblical *a priori* over-riding case for monogamous marriage.

19.4–11: +S

A gang rape. The men of Sodom want to gang rape Lot's angelic house guests. Lot's response, on the basis of hospitality, is to forestall this terrible event by offering his own daughters to be gang raped. The narrative implies some sympathy with Lot and the angels, and none at all with Lot's daughters. Any impartial reading of this text would see it as a commentary (though not as censorious as contemporary sensibility) on rape and not homosexuality *per se*. The only justification there can be for the subsequent massacre of all the women and children of Sodom as the punishment for whatever homosexuality there was can only be explained if women and children are moral pawns, the property of their men. As to the men themselves, Abraham's dialogue with the Lord (18.20–33) secures the promise that Sodom will not be destroyed if there are as few as ten righteous men in it, and so we must draw the conclusion, as it is destroyed, that there were fewer than ten. It is difficult to imagine any city where all but ten males are homosexual. It is difficult to see, with all this complexity, what moral the author is trying to draw, but this cannot in any way be accepted as a commentary on domestic homosexual relationships. It is only included as relevant because it is one of the few references to homosexuality which are aggregated to make the case against all homosexual relations.

19.31–38: -S
Incest to preserve Lot's hereditary line recounted without negative comment.

22.14: -S
Nahor's concubine introduced without negative comment. The question might arise whether the sexual practises of Genesis represent a pre-Covenant state of moral looseness but this construal is weak on two counts. First, concubines persisted without comment after Moses; secondly, the Genesis text was almost certainly written in the 7th or 6th Century BCE at which time the writers could have commented negatively on behaviour without being unfaithful to their narrative.

28.9: -S
Esau's polygamy noted without comment.

29.21–30.21: -S
 Sexual hi-jinks between Jacob and two sisters, Leah and Rachel, and their respective maids account for the strange circumstances by which twelve tribes were created. This looks like yet another example of any notional sexual ethics being subject to higher considerations, in this case the establishment of the tribal system.

34: -S
Dinah's rape condemned and avenged, but is this a matter of family honour rather than sexual ethics?

38.8–10: -S

Onan is bound to marry his dead brother's widow Tamar (Levirate marriage to protect widows) and is killed for ejaculating outside her. Again, surely a dynastic issue which raises the question of how far this edict against birth control can apply today; in any case, this surely cannot be an edict against masturbation where a wife is not proximate.

35.22: -S

Reuben sleeps with Bilhah, Jacob's concubine and Rachel's maid, and is apparently, therefore, deprived of primogeniture (cf. 49.4). However, this rule is frequently abridged: cf. Isaac's accidental preference for Jacob over Esau in Chapter 25 and Jacob's deliberate preference, in spite of Joseph's objection, for the younger Ephraim over the older Manasseh in Chapter 48. Indeed, given the lengths to which God is prepared to go to first instigate and then overcome barrenness to assert his power and propagate Abraham's dynasty, the lengths to which his descendants are prepared, or even forced, to go to preserve the dynastic structure, are quite remarkable and can in no wise be taken as templates for contemporary instruction. This necessarily raises the question of what can be taken as instructive when so much has to be rejected. Are we not in danger of framing our own sexual ethics and then foisting these on the Bible?

38.13–30: -S

Tamar tricks her father-in-law, Judah, into making her pregnant for dynastic reasons.

41.50: -S

Joseph marries the daughter of an Egyptian priest without negative comment in a passage which can be interpreted as adulatory. The Old Testament is deeply ambivalent about Jews marrying non-Jews; cf. Moses marrying a Cushite (often described as "Ethiopian"), cited without comment (Numbers 12.1), while Solomon's marrying many "foreign women" (1 Kings 11.1) is frowned upon. The over-riding principle is not ethnicity itself, but rather the extent to which ethnic diversity adversely affects religious loyalty.

49.4: -S
Reuben robbed of his birth right; cf. 35.22–23.

Summary

	S	-S	+S	P	-P	+P	J	-J	+J
Genesis	23	17	6	**0**	0	0	**0**	0	0

1.1.2. Exodus

In Exodus we move from 'primitive' and Patriarchal laws to codified Mosaic Law which carries more weight, although there is ample evidence that the formulations are much later than the time of Moses.

16: +P
The first reference to the distribution of resources. In this case the divine ordinance is that everybody receives a precisely identical amount of manna and storage/accumulation is forbidden.

20.14: +S
The first injunction against adultery. In this case it is a specific prohibition but the term 'adultery' is often used to represent all wrong-doing rather than specifically sexual sin (cf. the way in which modern English uses 'adulterate' to mean 'spoil' or 'contaminate'). It is important to determine whether the chief evil of adultery is seen as a property crime against the husband or whether it is a sexual misdemeanour.

20.15: +P
The injunction against stealing can be understood narrowly as forbidding an act of theft, removing the property of another, but it might be more widely understood as depriving somebody of what is rightfully theirs.

20.17: +P
Against covetousness, often downplayed in legal systems based on outcome.

21.2–11: -S
Concerns the treatment of slaves in respect of marriage, implying that the disposal of married slaves is fundamentally a matter of property rights.

21–2-21: +J

21.26–27: +J

21.32: +J
Rules of justice for slaves which strongly imply at least the same, if not more stringent, procedural justice for non-slaves.

22.16–17: -S
The economics of virginity; these are clearly property and not sexual issues.

22.21–29: +P
Economic justice for the weak, much more exacting than that which has applied in 'Western' judicial systems, emphasising the virtues of Mosaic Law over systems designed by Christians.

23.3–6: +P
Justice for the poor re-affirmed.

23.9: +P
Against the oppression of aliens, particularly relevant during controversy over UK immigration policy.

23.10–11: +P
The seventh year for the poor. Even though this refers to a rural economy, nothing like it has been developed as an equivalent for industrial or post-industrial society; another example of the superiority of Mosaic over contemporary socio-economic arrangements.

Summary

	S	-S	+S	P	-P	+P	J	-J	+J
Exodus	3	2	1	7	0	7	3	0	3

1.1.3.   Leviticus

In spite of its name, it is important to take careful note of where ordinances refer to the people as a whole rather than specifically to priests.

18.6–18: -S
Against the nakedness of kin. It might seem odd to give this topic such importance but the text strongly implies that to see somebody naked is tantamount to having sexual relations with them.

18.19: -S
Against nakedness during menstruation. We have already seen the fusing of sexual and economic issues; this is the first instance of a comparable fusion between the issues of purity and sexual activity.

18.22: +S
An unequivocal condemnation of homosexuality, which is described as an "abomination" and put on a par with sexual relations with animals. The brevity of the injunction and its proximity to that concerning animals can be explained by the low possibility or incidence of the occurrence. In spite of some authors surmising that lesbian behaviour was rife among the many wives and concubines of a single man, the prospect of lesbianism is not acknowledged here or anywhere else.re or anywhere else.[2]

19.9–20: +P
Enjoins a deliberate policy of leaving the edges of land unreaped, and leaving grain and grapes to be gleaned by the poor and the alien. This is the equivalent of a redistributive taxation policy which affords more dignity than the workhouse; cf. the Book of Ruth.

19.13: +P
Against fraud and sharp dealing; the first is legally obvious but the second is significant in view of numerous instances of sharp dealing. C Compare with the deception of Isaac in Genesis 27 and the intoxication and 'rape' of Lot in Genesis 19.31–38 whicht are apparently condoned by the author as necessary, for example, for dynastic survival. What might be permissible in the dynastic sphere is not permissible in the economic sphere.

19.15: +J
Requires equal procedural justice for all people.

19.19: +P
The first citation of the golden rule: love your neighbour as yourself.

---

[2]   See, for example, Richard Elliott Friedman and Shawna Dolansky, *The Bible Now* (Oxford University Press, 2011).

19.20–22: -S
Against sexual relations with another person's slave girl; another instance of sex being equated with property law.

19.29: +S
Against female prostitution. Although we will see some equivocation on this point elsewhere – notably in the case of Rahab in Joshua 2.1–21, 6.17, and 6.22–23.5, perhaps because she is not of the Chosen People – this particular reference is unequivocal.

19.33–34: +P
The protection of aliens has recently become an important ethical issue because of the move in many rich countries to vilify all aliens and immigrants as a class.

19.35–36: +P
Requires honest trading.

20.10: +S
The death penalty required for adultery with the wife of a neighbour. While the sentence is not relevant it clearly demonstrates the perceived gravity of this act. .

20.13: +S
The punishment for homosexuality is the same as that for adultery. On the one hand, nothing can be more severe than death. On the other, we need to consider whether the two cases should be treated equally when many Christians who unequivocally condemn homosexuality nevertheless support re-marriage after divorce; an act which, at the very least, involves one partner in adultery and often both. -. We will see a great deal more emphasis on the sin of adultery rather than on homosexuality, but that might be because the former is more likely and because it involves issues of property but the question of equal treatment is still open.

20.14–21: -S
Against a variety of unacceptable sexual practices, concerning incest and impurity.

21.7: -S
Priests must not marry prostitutes, divorcees, or non-virgins.

21.8: -S
A priest's daughter should not become a prostitute. What about the daughters of the laity?

21.13–15: -S
Priests must marry virgins from their own tribe.

25.13–17: +P
Fairness is required during the jubilee year; a truly life-changing event for the poor, and particularly for slaves, with the remission of debts and the granting of freedom.

25.35–43: +P
The importance of the care of impoverished dependents strikes a jarring note in a society of nuclear families, particularly with respect to the aged.

25.46: +J
Against harsh rule.

25.53: +J
Against the harsh rule of aliens.

Summary

	S	-S	+S	P	-P	+P	J	-J	+J
Leviticus	11	7	4	7	0	7	3	0	3

1.1.4.   Numbers

Like Exodus, this fourth book of the *Pentateuch* mixes narrative with legal provisions, but these are quite narrow and none of them apply to us today.

5.11–15: -S
Penalties for actual or supposed female marital infidelity; recognises the sin of jealousy.

5.20–27: -S
 A woman is cursed with infertility for adultery; an injunction which would seem to negate restitution for adultery as an infertile woman is useless to the husband in this culture and it is therefore tantamount to the option of divorce. Male marital adultery is not mentioned.

12: -S
Moses marries a Cushite woman, which apparently contradicts injunctions against marrying foreigners, cf. 25.1–5. However, the point seems not to be ethnicity *per se,* but rather the extent to which foreign wives (not spouses) induce adultery: yet another variant on the general theme of women, supposedly morally weaker, being held responsible for the misdeeds of men.

25.1–9: -S
Against marrying Moabites or Midianites.

27.1–8: -S
The women of Zelopheth are allowed to inherit, if there are no brothers, for dynastic reasons.

30: -S
The vow of a woman subject to their father and/or husband.

31.17–18: -S

Women, except virgins who are spoils of conquest, are included in genocidal edicts, not dissimilar to their blameless annihilation in Genesis 19.

Summary

	S	-S	+S	P	-P	+P	J	-J	+J
Numbers	7	7	0	0	0	0	0	0	0

1.1.5. Deuteronomy

The *Pentateuch* concludes with the most powerful of its five books, in which history and law are most closely integrated. We will see that on some points it is much more liberal than our materialist and punitive society, whereas on other points it calls for far more brutality than any punishment we would envisage. In general, there is a good deal of legislation relating to sex and gender which we would regard as irrelevant,, but a good deal of economic and social legislation that we would consider applicable to us. Hence, although there are more sexual references (S) than those applying to power and wealth (P), the relevance count of these two categories is almost identical.

1.16–17: +J

Impartial justice for all.

5.18: +S

You shall not commit adultery; not quite as straightforward as it might seem; cf. Exodus 20.4. It seems, from reading the text between this and the Exodus listing of the Commandments, that women are punished for adultery and blamed for male adultery. This turns out not to be precisely the case, cf. 22.22, but there is still a strong sense of pro-male bias.

5.19: +P

Injunction against stealing; cf. Exodus 20.15. Although detailed regulations are clear about direct theft there is also a deep sense of what is a person's due.

5.21: +P

Against covetousness; cf. Exodus 20.17. A particularly interesting injunction because it is not 'outcome' based but refers to an intention or motive.

15.1–6: +P

A remission of debt every seven years, fascinating because it is such a liberal provision which would not be countenanced in our more 'civilised' culture. Indeed, one of the features that emerges in Deuteronomy is how 'liberal' its laws are compared with, say, sixteenth-century England or even, in some respects, England today. Since this law did not apply to non-Jews and because Medieval Christians were also not supposed to practise usury, Christians borrowed money from Jews and then hypocritically blamed them for the imposition. We might argue that such a provision would not be possible today because it would not allow for long-term lending for house purchasing but, again, it presses hard on the 'literal' methodology of understanding the text. Underlying this position there is a further issue which applies to much of the law we are considering: the legislator specifically applies law to the Chosen People and excludes non-Jews from it, so why should we, as non-Jews, choose to include ourselves in provisions from which we were specifically excluded? By extension, this raises the issue of the criteria by which we have excluded ourselves from food, purity, and adultery provisions but retained that provision concerning homosexuality. We might cogently argue that the first two are *de minimis*, but our official Christian re-marriage provision requires careful consideration even if the adultery is sequential rather than parallel.

15.7–11: +P
Lend liberally or make a gift to the needy.

15.12–18: -J
Be humane to slaves.

20.7: -S
A marriage must be consummated before a warrior goes into battle, yet another example of the human nature of these laws.

20.14: -S
Women to be included in war booty, another problem for literalists.

21.10–14: -S
On the treatment of captive women.

<u>22.5: +S</u>
Against cross-dressing which is "abhorrent to the Lord your God"; quite why is not clear but perhaps there is a sense that the cross dresser is homosexual.. Again, because it is pertinent to the sub-topic of homosexuality, I have marked this as a key passage.

22.13–21: -S
A discourse on male gratification and redress. In this strange passage, it is envisaged that a man who dislikes his new wife may accuse her of not being a nuptial virgin in order to slander her. If a bride proves not to be a virgin she must be stoned to death. There is, of course, no reference to male nuptial virginity.

22.22: +S
The stoning of both parties to an adultery, scored relevant not because of the sentence but because of the seriousness attached to the deed. In this rare case both parties are equally punished.

22.23–27: +S
Stoning for sex with an engaged woman, with an interesting standard of proof where the woman is only found guilty of collusion, rather than being the victim of a rape, if the event takes place within human ear-shot.

22.28–29: -S
Fornication with a non-betrothed woman triggers marriage. This is interesting because it makes a clear distinction between the violation of a property right in adultery, cf. 22.22, and a non-property right in fornication.

22.30: -S
Against marrying a father's wife.

23.1: -S
The exclusion of genitally damaged males from public life emphasises the centrality of sexual relations.

23.2: -S
Bastards socially excluded for ten generations.

23.17–18: -S
Israelites shall not be female or male temple prostitutes and any fees from prostitution may not be used in payment at the House of the Lord. The degree to which this applies to non-Israelites is questionable; cf. 15.1–6.

23.19: -P
Usury should not be practised on Jews; cf. 15.1–6.

23.24–25: -P
You may eat casually of your neighbour's crops but not carry food away in containers, another humane precept.

24.1–4: -S
A man may not re-marry his divorced wife.

24.13: -P
Limits on the enforcement of pledges, another humane example.

24.15–16: +P
On the prompt payment of wages to Jews and aliens.

24.17–18: +J
On the dispensation of justice to the poor.

24.19–22: +P
cf. Leviticus 19.19–20.

25.5–20: -S
The codification of the rule that a man must marry his deceased brother's wife (Levirate marriage) to preserve the dynasty (cf. Genesis 38.18–20), but also to afford protection to the widow. This is one sexual provision we have abandoned.

25.11–12: -S
A woman who protects her husband in a fight by grabbing the genitals of his opponent will have her hand cut off.

27.17: +P
One of the 'Twelve curses', against moving a boundary marker which is the highest form of theft in an agrarian economy.

27.19: +P
Another curse, this time for those who withhold justice from the poor.

27.2–23: -S
Curses against various forms of sexual infraction but not, significantly, as sex with animals is included, a curse against homosexuality.

Summary

	S	-S	+S	P	-P	+P	J	-J	+J
Deuteronomy	17	13	4	11	3	8	3	1	2

Conclusion

	S	-S	+S	P	-P	+P	J	-J	+J
Genesis	23	17	6	0	0	0	0	0	0
Exodus	3	2	1	7	0	7	3	0	3
Leviticus	11	7	4	7	0	7	3	0	3
Numbers	7	7	0	0	0	0	0	0	0
Deuteronomy	17	13	4	11	3	8	3	1	2
TOTAL	61	46	15	25	3	22	9	1	8

Although there are more than twice as many sex and gender references compared with those for power and wealth, the relevant references of the latter are half as much again as those for the former. Relevant procedural justice references are half of those for sex and gender.

1.2. THE NARRATIVES

Although there are some legal pronouncements, we largely learn about our three clusters of concerns in these narratives from what people say and do. As the narratives are largely about the relationship between God and 'his' people in terms of 'political'/ theocratic leadership, there are far fewer references than in the law-dominated Pentateuch.

1.2.1. Joshua

The first part of the Book of Joshua tells the story of the Chosen People's entry and partial occupation of the 'Promised Land'; the second part largely concerns the allocation of land to the Twelve Tribes.

2.1–21: -S
The collaboration between Jewish spies and the prostitute Rahab. Her 'profession' is never condemned, perhaps because she is not of the Chosen people, or perhaps simply because she is being useful.

6.17: -S
The promise of immunity from the ravages of conquest for Rahab and her family is confirmed.

6.21: -S
No combatants, including women, are slaughtered.

6.22–23, 25: -S
The promise to Rahab confirmed.

23.12–14: -S
Against marriage with foreigners.

Summary

	S	-S	+S	P	-P	+P	J	-J	+J
Joshua	5	5	0	0	0	0	0	0	0

1.2.2. Judges

The Book of Judges describes a chaotic period in which "All the people did what was right in their own eyes" (14.6, 21.25). Periods of faithfulness and political calm alternate with periods of unfaithfulness and foreign oppression.

4: -S
The rule of Deborah as a judge cited without negative comment.

4.17–21: -S
The heroism of Jael again narrated without negative comment.

5.30: -S
"A girl or two for every man" as part of the spoils of victory.

8.30–31: -S
Gideon had seventy sons and many wives and concubines; apparently adulatory. There are numerous references in Judges which contradict the contemporary notion that the Bible states that marriage is between one man and one woman, e.g. 10.3–4, 12.8–10, 12.13–15.

11.1–2: -S
Jephtha, by virtue of being the son of a prostitute, cannot inherit.

11.34–40: -S
Jephtha's daughter sacrificed before which she bemoans her virginity. Unlike Isaac (Genesis 22.1–14) she is not reprieved.

14.1–15.8: -S
The complexities of marriage between Sampson and a non-Jew.

16.1–4: -S
Sampson consorts with a prostitute without negative comment, perhaps because she is a non-Jew; but he is not!

19: -S[3]
The strange and terrible story of the gang rape and murder of the Levite's concubine. This story echoes Genesis 19.4–11. The Levite's concubine and his host's virgin daughter are offered to a crowd in place of the Levite. Although the depraved men are characterised as homosexuals, the sacrifice of the woman would seem to be on the grounds of hospitality. Either way, the proposed gang rape of the guest bears no relation to contemporary domestic homosexual relationships any more than we can claim the authority of Scripture for the gang rape of a woman. The Levite blames the crowd and takes no personal responsibility for his action. Unlike Genesis 19.4–11, where it is not clear whether the women offered for rape were violated, the Levite's concubine was certainly raped to death; a strange proceeding for allegedly homosexual men.

20.48: -S
In a further parallel with Genesis 19, the Benjamite women are murdered because of the threatened homosexual gang rape of the Levite and the actual gang rape of his concubine.

21.10–12: -S
The women of Jabeshgilead murdered except for virgins who are distributed as property; cf. 20.40.

21.20–24: -S
The women of Shiloh are abducted for sinful Benjamin.

---

[3]   Underlined because this passage requires detailed and careful consideration.

Summary

	S	-S	+S	P	-P	+P	J	-J	+J
Judges	12	12	0	0	0	0	0	0	0

1.2.3. Ruth

The Book of Ruth is a glowing confirmation of the precepts of the *Pentateuch* lived out faithfully. It emphasises the importance of caring for the poor, particularly those of one's family.

1.8–13: -S
Confirmation of Levirate Marriage.

2: +P
The importance of making provision for gleaning, cf. Leviticus 19.9–20.

Summary

	S	-S	+S	P	-P	+P	J	-J	+J
Ruth	17	13	4	11	3	8	3	1	2

1.2.4. 1 Samuel

The First Book of Samuel describes the emergence of a monarchy for the Chosen People, opposed by the priest and prophet Samuel but reluctantly accepted and then regretted by God. Although it lacks any strong ethical current, it contains some striking indicators.

2.1–10: +P
Hannah's prayer of thanksgiving for the gift of her son, Samuel, contains a sustained and striking confirmation of the Lord's obligations to, and protection of, the poor and weak. These verses prefigure the thanksgiving prayer of Mary the mother of Jesus for her own pregnancy; cf. Luke 1.46–55. Hannah is the first fully-drawn woman in the Old Testament. Her character is more rounded, for example, than Rebekah, whom we first meet properly at Genesis 25.15, or Rachel at Genesis 29.7—who is initially treated in her plea to be relieved from being barren as a drunkard. However, the love Rachel's husband Elkanah shows to her over his more fertile wife Peninnah, and her steadfast gratitude shown in her annual visits to Samuel and his protégée Eli the Priest, demonstrates that not all authors typecast women as any combination of fools, seductresses, or mere foetus carriers. It is also highly significant that, considering the overall burden of the Old Testament texts, such a strong pronouncement on justice should be made by a woman.

2.22: +S
Elkanah condemns the adultery of his sons Hophne and Phinehas.

2.4–5: -S
Men considered being ritually unclean after sexual intercourse.

27.9: -S
David slaughters women as well as men.

25.44: -S
Saul takes David's wife Michal and gives her to another man; presumably for dynastic reasons but perhaps simply out of personal spite, typifying his deeply ambivalent attitude to David.

Summary

	S	-S	+S	P	-P	+P	J	-J	+J
1 Samuel	4	3	1	1	0	1	0	0	0

1.2.5.   2 Samuel

The Second Book of Samuel is largely concerned with the reign of the Priest/King David of Bethlehem. Its sexual references point to a sharp distinction between the permitted behaviour of monarchs and the legal sanctions set out in Deuteronomy. This poses further questions about the use of Old Testament narrative as a contemporary ethical guide.

2.15–16: -S
David reclaims his former wife Michal in spite of the prohibition on re-marriage after divorce; cf. Deuteronomy 24.1–4.

6.23: -S
Barrenness as a punishment. Up until this point it has simply been a misfortune.

11.11–25: +S
David adulterously seduces Bathsheba and attempts to conceal his wrong-doing by murdering her husband. Neither party is stoned for this adultery in spite of the demands of Deuteronomy 22.22, and, although Bathsheba loses the resulting child, she goes on to produce David's favoured son and successor, Solomon.

12.1–12: +P
The prophet Nathan spells out the social obligations flouted by David's adultery in the touching story of the small holder and his single lamb.

13: -S
Ammon rapes his sister Tamar. He is not judicially punished but killed as an act of revenge.

26.21–22: -S
The rebel Absalom, son of David, rapes ten of his father's concubines, but the remaining religious authorities in Jerusalem take no action against him.

20.4: -S
David makes a settlement on the raped concubines but they are punished by his rejection of them.

Summary

	S	-S	+S	P	-P	+P	J	-J	+J
2 Samuel	6	5	1	1	0	1	0	0	0

1.2.6.   1 Kings

The First Book of the Kings continues the history of the combined monarchy of Judea and Israel under Solomon before it divides on traditional lines at his death. The majority of sexual references concern male prostitutes, apparently in idolatrous places of worship.

1.1–4: -S
With the loss of sexual potency, David loses political potency.

3.1: -S
Solomon marries Pharaoh's daughter with apparent authorial approval; contrast with 11.1 below.

1.16–28: -S
In the course of Solomon's famous judgment on the disputed maternity of a son between two prostitutes, there is no condemnation of their 'profession' even though they appear not to be foreigners as Solomon is consulted in the case. This seems to confirm a general indifference to prostitution, in sharp contrast to the seriousness of adultery, which is itself primarily a property infraction rather than a sexual misdeed.

11.1–13: -S
Condemnation of Solomon's foreign women, because of their idolatry not their number.

14.24: -S

15.12: -S
Male temple prostitutes are deemed abominable and cleared out of the land; they appear to be foreigners but it is not clear whether they serve women or are homosexual.

22.38: -S
Prostitutes wash in the pool where the assassinated King Ahab's blood flows; detestation by association.

22.46: -S
Remnant of male temple prostitutes killed; again, apparently in idolatrous places of worship.

Summary

	S	-S	+S	P	-P	+P	J	-J	+J
1 Kings	8	8	0	0	0	0	0	0	0

1.2.7. 2 Kings

The two kingdoms of Judea and Israel weaken and grow further apart, until Israel and then Judea are over-run and their people taken into exile. The only remarkable incident is the accession by the female Athaliah to the Judean throne, apparently without trouble and certainly without authorial comment in respect of her gender; the objections to her are solely on the grounds of her character.

11.1: -S
Athaliah rules Judea without objection or comment on the grounds of her gender. This, much more than the temporary and ramshackle leadership of Deborah (cf. Judges 4), puts Genesis 3.16 into serious doubt as a text against female dominance in the public sphere. It is important to distinguish between the condemnation of her character and the silence over her right to reign.

23.7: -S
The clearing out of apparently idolatrous male prostitutes.

Summary

	S	-S	+S	P	-P	+P	J	-J	+J
2 Kings	2	2	0	0	0	0	0	0	0

1.2.8. 1 Chronicles

The two Books of the Chronicles cover much of the ground of the two books of the Kings but with a slightly less pro-Judean slant, so we can expect many of the same events to be narrated and the same passages cited, which proves to be the case.

4.17: -S
Mered married Bithiah daughter of Pharaoh.

5.1–2: -S
Reuben robbed of his birth right; cf. Genesis 35.22–23, 49.4.

Summary

	S	-S	+S	P	-P	+P	J	-J	+J
1 Chronicles	2	2	0	0	0	0	0	0	0

1.2.9.   2 Chronicles

The story of the Judean and Israel dynasties continues towards final disaster.

8.11: -S
Solomon's Egyptian wife is not to live in any place where the Ark of the Lord has been.

22.9–12: -S
The reign of Athaliah; cf. 2 Kings 11.

Summary

	S	-S	+S	P	-P	+P	J	-J	+J
2 Chronicles	2	2	0	0	0	0	0	0	0

1.2.10. Esther

The Book of Esther describes a Jewish virgin becoming the favourite wife of non-Jewish Emperor Ahasuerus. The narrative presents two apparently bewildering propositions: first, that a woman can be resourceful and heroic; secondly, that an Emperor can assemble as massive a harem of wives and concubines as he pleases, including Jewish virgins. On the second point, although there seems to be Old Testament equivocation about Jewish males marrying non-Jewish females, the same prohibition does not seem to apply to non-Jewish males marrying Jewish females. Perhaps the provision is not general but is justified by how Esther uses her position to save her people from genocide, another example of pragmatism overriding ethical theory. . Perhaps, too, royalty is permitted to abide by a different code of sexual ethics for dynastic reasons. Incidentally, it is often asserted that the Book of Esther has no references to God, but this is only true in this case because key extracts of the book are only included in the Greek Version (cf. Greek Esther, below).

2.2–4: -S
A multiplicity of young virgins is brought to the king, without authorial comment.

2.18: -S
Esther the Jewess is brought to the emperor without comment.

2.12–17: -S
The emperor 'tries' a succession of virgins to see which he likes, without comment.

Summary

	S	-S	+S	P	-P	+P	J	-J	+J
Esther	3	3	0	0	0	0	0	0	0

1.2.11. Ezra

The book of Ezra concerns the return to Judea of exiles from Babylon permitted by the new Persian regime.

10: -S
Against foreign wives.

Summary

	S	-S	+S	P	-P	+P	J	-J	+J
Ezra	1	1	0	0	0	0	0	0	0

1.2.12. Nehemiah

A parallel story to that of Ezra about the return of the exiles.

5.1–13: +P
Against usury and economic oppression

9.32: +J
The "terrible" God of mercy.

13.26–27: -S
Against foreign wives.

Summary

	S	-S	+S	P	-P	+P	J	-J	+J
Nehemiah	1	1	0	1	0	1	1	0	1

Conclusion

	S	-S	+S	P	-P	+P	J	-J	+J
Joshua	5	5	0	0	0	0	0	0	0
Judges	12	12	0	0	0	0	0	0	0
Ruth	1	1	0	1	0	1	0	0	0
1 Samuel	4	3	1	1	0	1	0	0	0
2 Samuel	6	5	1	1	0	1	0	0	0
1 Kings	8	8	0	0	0	0	0	0	0
2 Kings	2	2	0	0	0	0	0	0	0
1 Chronicles	2	2	0	0	0	0	0	0	0
2 Chronicles	2	2	0	0	0	0	0	0	0
Esther	3	3	0	0	0	0	0	0	0
Ezra	1	1	0	0	0	0	0	0	0
Nehemiah	1	1	0	1	0	1	1	0	1
TOTAL	47	45	2	4	0	4	1	0	1

At first glance the analysis of the narratives looks like a futile exercise: there are hardly any references to power and wealth, nor to procedural justice. The references to sexual conduct are almost entirely irrelevant to our discussion, concentrating on dynastic sexual conduct, polygamy and concubinage. What emerges, however, is a striking confirmation of one of my initial assumptions to be investigated; namely that ethical behaviour is not the prime concern of the Bible.

1.3. WISDOM LITERATURE

The most familiar element in the Wisdom literature is the Book of Psalms which is the backbone of daily Christian prayer. The Book of Job offers some insights into our investigation but its major concerns lie elsewhere. The Book of Proverbs is a rag-bag of nostrums.

1.3.1.   Job

The Book of Job is primarily concerned with the life of righteousness under critical challenge, both from Job's circumstances and his supposed friends. There is a strong vein of socio-economic justice and a strong advocacy of marital fidelity.

The text is markedly rhetorical, operating as a set of test cases or 'diatribes' which means that it is vital to distinguish between direct statement and irony; a perfect example of the difference between adducing the plain meaning of the text and taking each statement in the text literally.

2.20: -S
The association of foolishness and women.

5.15: +P
The Lord saves the needy from the mighty and gives them hope, as should we.

22.5–12: +P
Condemns the oppression of the poor.

24: +P, +S
Wickedness defined in terms of economic oppression; adultery is part of that wickedness.

29.12–17: +P
Virtue defined socio-economically

30.24–25: +P
The plight of the needy.

31.9–12: +S
Marital faithfulness affirmed.

31.16–28, 32: +P
Wickedness defined socio-economically.

Summary

	S	-S	+S	P	-P	+P	J	-J	+J
Job	3	1	2	6	0	6	0	0	0

1.3.2. Psalms

The Book of Psalms is traditionally supposed to have been composed by King David. There is ample evidence that this cannot be the case and that the poems were written over a long period; some before David and some as late as the 6th Century exile of the Judeans in Babylon.

As we would expect from a book of texts calling on the Lord, there is a recognition of his role in achieving social and procedural justice. I rate these references positively because they say that, by extension, we should imitate the Lord. It is sometimes difficult to distinguish between socio-economic and procedural justice.

10: +P, +J
An essay against oppression of the poor by the powerful which the Lord will avenge.

12.5: +P
"The proud will rise up" because "the poor are despoiled and the needy groan"; a rhetorical condemnation of the proud.

14.6: +P
The wicked wish to confound the poor but the Lord is their refuge.

33.5: +J
The Lord loves righteousness and justice; I take this to mean procedural rather than socio-economic justice.

37.1–22: +P
The wicked bring down the poor and needy.

37.28: +J
The Lord loves justice.

41.1: +P
Happy are those who consider the poor.

50.17: +S
Disparagement of the adulterous.

62.9: +P
Do not set your heart on riches.

68.6: +P
The Lord gives a home to the desolate.

73.12: +P
The wicked increase in riches.

74.12–22: +P
Do not let the down-trodden be put to shame; rise up, Lord, and remember how the impious scoff at you.

82.3–4: +P, +J
Give justice to the weak and the orphan; maintain the right of the lowly and destitute; rescue the weak and the needy from the wicked.

94.15: -J
(Divine) justice will return to the righteous.

103.6: +J
The Lord brings about justice for the oppressed.

107.9: +P
(The Lord) satisfies the thirsty and hungry, perhaps figurative of spiritual needs.

112.5: +P, +J
It is well for those who deal generously and justly.

146.7–9: +J
The Lord dispenses justice and so, by extension, should we.

147.6: +P
The Lord uplifts the down-trodden.

Summary

	S	-S	+S	P	-P	+P	J	-J	+J
Psalms	1	0	1	14	0	14	7	1	6

1.3.3. Proverbs

The Book of Proverbs is a loosely organised collection of sayings attributed to Solomon (cf. 1 Kings 1–11). It is characterised by some pithy aphorisms but also often by a lazy, conventional misogyny. As we would expect, it has much to say about all three of our subjects. If the socio-economic aphorisms are taken literally, cf. 23.10, then there is much here that does not apply to us; I believe that it is hardly contentious to understand meaning by extension here as this is wisdom rather than 'Law' which might be taken much more literally. We should notice, apart from the misogyny, that most of the comments on sexual behaviour are against adultery.

1.3: +J
Righteousness, justice, and equity constitute wise dealing.

2.16–19: +S
Against adultery.

5: -S
Beware the loose woman. To avoid repetition, this is one of many passages which characterises loose sexual morals as arising from the seduction by women rather than the lack of male self-control, an argument which characterises contemporary debate about 'provocative' female attire as a mitigating factor in rape, and also the key designator behind the Islamic stricture on female attire to save males from provocation.

6.24–35: +S
Against adultery.

7: +S
Against adultery.

9.13: -S
The foolish woman is loud.

11.1: +P
Against cheating.

11.4: +P
Righteousness above riches.

11.22: -S
Good sense over beauty. A sentiment which might appear sensible in its way, but which clearly extends its hostility to corporeal female beauty as opposed to, say, an architectural work.

11.24–28: +P

In praise of generosity.

12.4: -S

In praise of the good wife. Instructive, although this does not relate directly to our enquiry. For this reason, and not because I am against good wives, it receives a minus score.

13.11: -P

Wealth hastily gained will dwindle. Scored minus because this is purely utilitarian.

14.21: +P

Happy are those who are kind to the poor.

14.31: +P

Those who oppress the poor insult their creator.

15.16–18: -P

The consolations of the poor.

15.25: +P

The Lord maintains the widow's boundaries, and so should we in a contemporary context.

15.27: -P

Those who are greedy make trouble for their own household; utilitarian rather than principled.

16.8: +P

Better a little paired with righteousness than much paired with injustice.

16.11: -P

In praise of honest balances, although since this might be extended to 'pay day lending' I have scored it minus.

16.19: +P
Better to be lowly among the poor than divide the spoil of the proud. This, and similar, would come better from a poor philosopher than a rich and magnificent king, but we have to take the sayings at face value.

17.23: +J
Against bribery in justice, scored plus because it extends to interference in procedural justice by the rich and powerful.

18.5: +J
In praise of impartial justice.

19.13: -S
A wife's quarrelling is like dripping rain. He does not add that a man's anger is like a thunderstorm!

19.17: +P
Whoever is kind to the poor lends to the Lord.

21.3: +J
Justice is better than ritual sacrifice.

21.9: -S
The contentious wife.

21.10: +J
There is no mercy in the wicked.

21.13: +P
If you close your ears to the poor, the Lord will close his ears to you.

21.15: +J
Justice is joy to the righteous.

21.19: -S
Against the contentious wife.

21.21: +P
The righteous and kind will receive honour.

22.1: -P
A good name is better than riches; utilitarian.

22.8: -J
Whoever sows justice will reap calamity; utilitarian.

22.9: +P
The generous are blessed.

22.14: -S
The mouth of a loose woman is a deep pit. Seduction is indeed a terrible trap but scores minus because of the absence of a countervailing aphorism about men.

22.16: -P
Oppressing the poor will bring loss. A nice balance of principle and utilitarianism; scored minus.

22.22–23: +P
Do not oppress the poor; apparently utilitarian but carries a divine sanction.

23.10: +P
Do not encroach on the fields of orphans; cf. comment on the Book of Job as a whole, above.

23.27–28: +S
Against prostitution and adultery.

25.24: -S
The contentious wife; again.

28.15: -S
The contentious wife; cf. 19.13. We get the message!

29.6: +P
Better to be poor and straight than rich and crooked.

30.3: -S
Against prostitution; scored minus because not relevant to our enquiry.

30.14: +J
A king should rule the poor with equity, taken here to mean procedural justice.

31.20: +S
Against adultery, but blamed on the woman.

32.3: -S
Against succumbing to women.

32.8: +P
Speak out for those who cannot speak.

Summary

	S	-S	+S	P	-P	+P	J	-J	+J
Proverbs	17	12	5	22	6	16	8	1	7

1.3.4. Ecclesiastes

The Book of Ecclesiastes (not to be confused with Ecclesiasticus in the Apocrypha) is also supposed to have been written by King Solomon. It is a world-weary book for a king and its rhetoric is somewhat contrived, which means that it is even more important than in the Book of Job to distinguish between irony and direct statement.

2.8: -S
Praise of the delights of the flesh and many concubines. To be contrasted with Solomon's frequent advice against the same, cf. Proverbs, but also contrary to his apparent lifestyle, cf. 1 Kings 1–11.

7.26–29: -S
Lazy misogyny extended to all women, not just the foolish or beautiful.

9.9: +S
In praise of the uxorious; note this is couched in the singular in spite of 1 Kings 11.1.

10.19: -P
In praise of money, apparently against all his other advice.

Summary

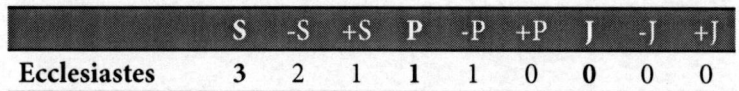

	S	-S	+S	P	-P	+P	J	-J	+J
Ecclesiastes	3	2	1	1	1	0	0	0	0

1.3.5.   Song of Songs

The Song of Songs, also apparently written by Solomon, paradoxically says nothing about sexual values although we might suppose it to be in favour of marriage. The eroticism is frequently down-played through oblique, and in some cases blatantly dishonest, translation. The scoring on all points is zero.

Conclusion

	S	-S	+S	P	-P	+P	J	-J	+J
Job	3	1	2	6	0	6	0	0	0
Psalms	1	0	1	14	0	14	7	1	6
Proverbs	17	12	5	22	6	16	8	1	7
Ecclesiastes	3	2	1	1	1	0	0	0	0
Song of Songs	0	0	0	0	0	0	0	0	0
TOTAL	24	15	9	43	7	36	15	2	13

In this series of books, socio-economic justice scores higher in general than either sexual issues or procedural justice in a ratio of roughly 7 : 4 : 2. However, when we look at the scores for positive references the ratios are: 7 : 3 : 2, and in the case of the last of these all references are either in favour of marriage and against adultery, and/or condemn prostitution.

1.4.   THE PROPHETS

The following seventeen books comprise six major prophets (the first six) and twelve minor prophets, with Lamentations sandwiched between Jeremiah and Ezekiel, and often erroneously attributed to the former. . The material spans a period of approximately 700 years, but most of it was written between 600 and 200 BCE. As the critical topics in the texts are the wickedness of the Chosen People, their prophetically proclaimed just punishment in exile, and the new hope of a yet vaguely perceived Messiah, we can expect deep introspection on the nature of the wickedness. This is almost entirely attributed to idolatry although, as we will see, there is some element of regret at social injustice.

Some of the minor prophets make no references to our enquiry and will be listed in the Conclusion with zero scores.

1.4.1.　Isaiah

Isaiah is by far the most passionate and consistent advocate of justice in the Old Testament. The book collectively known as Isaiah was probably written by three different authors or 'schools', the first in the seventh century BCE, before the exile of Judea in the sixth century BCE. The last was probably written near or just after the end of the exile. Isaiah is the most directly quoted prophet in the Gospels, and there are a number of references underlined here because of the significance Christians assign to them. It is perhaps the prophets' very passion for social and procedural justice, and their apparent indifference to legalism, which accounts for their relative lack of popularity.

1.17: +P, +J
Do good; seek justice; rescue the oppressed.

1.21: +J
"She (Jerusalem) that was full of justice . . . now murders."

1.23: +P, +J
Princes take bribes and do not defend the weak (widows and orphans).

1.27: -J
Zion will be redeemed by justice. We might, by extension, apply this to ourselves but the link is too weak for a plus.

3.12: -S
A sign of despair that "women rule over" the people.

3.13: -J
The Lord judges. The widely held belief that the Lord judges does not negate the need for earthly justice—civil or theocratic—which must not be partial to the rich or powerful.

3.14–15: +J
The powerful condemned for greed and oppression of the "vineyard".

3.16–24: +P
Against female adornment. This might have been scored -S but the context is greed in which males have been condemned for playing the greater part.

4.1: -S
The desperate plight of abandoned women, or condemnation of decadence.

4.4: -S
"Once the Lord has washed away the filth of the daughters of Zion" appears to characterise them in generic rather than gender terms.

5.16: +J
"The Lord of Hosts is exalted by justice".

5.23: +J
It is wrong to take bribes and deprive the innocent of their rights.

7.14: -S

"The young woman is with child and will bear a son . . . " Many Christians believe that this text foretells the virgin birth of Jesus. The issue for us is not whether this is so but the implications of its being held so widely and so long by Christians. We have to ask ourselves what such a doctrine says about our attitudes to male sexuality. Is male sperm fundamentally less worthy than a female egg? Is Joseph somehow less worthy than Mary? Is sexual intercourse so fundamentally corrupt that it cannot cause the Incarnation to take place? Further, does this doctrine account in part for the dichotomy of the pure woman on the pedestal and the whore? The scoring of the text is in relation to its questions about male sexuality and not the virgin birth as it relates to Mary.

9.6–8: +P, +J

The Lord's kingdom of righteousness and justice achieved through a child, a key text for Christians who hold that it foretells the birth of Jesus and the manner of his kingdom. Taken in that context, it is not likely that the justice contemplated is strictly procedural but rather that it has the broader sense of equality, at least of concern and respect if not treatment. The scoring and reference is underlined because those likely to take the passage as a Messianic prophesy about Jesus are highly likely to be those who rank sexual matters (S) over power and wealth (P) and justice (J) to which this key passage refers.

10.1–4: +P, +J

Largely concerned with the importance of procedural justice, particularly laws that are unjust to the poor, but also contains a socio-economic element.

11.4: +J

Equity for the poor and meek.

16.5: +J

The throne of steadfast love occupied by a lover of justice.

19.16: -S
The Egyptians will be like women – a customary disparagement.

23.15–18: -S
An initial, equivocal, almost beautiful, use of the metaphor of a prostitute for the desolate city of Tyre but in a word-play wherein the usual conventional, derogatory meaning is restored.

25.4–5: +P
The Lord protects the poor; very fine weather metaphors.

26.5–6: +P
The humbling of the proud who have oppressed the poor.

28: +P, +J
Against corrupt leaders and injustice.

29.17–21: +P, +J
Reward for the poor and meek from the "Holy one of Israel".

32.1: +J
At the appointed time, princes will rule with justice.

32.5–8: +P
Equating foolishness and villainy, particularly in maltreatment of the poor.

32.9: -S
"Rise up, you women who are at ease." Definite ambivalence about women who are at ease: at one level they are expected to be at ease, yet are insulted for it, while at another they are resented for being any different.

33.15–17: +J
The rewards for just conduct.

35.3–6: +P
A famous passage about the comfort that "The Lord" will bring, avenging those who have mistreated the poor and weak. Further, infirmities will be cured.

40.29: +P
The Lord empowers the powerless.

42.1–4: +P
"The servant" will bring justice.

51.5: +J
(The Lord's) justice as a light.

56.1: +J
An exhortation to maintain justice.

58.3–10: +P, +J
A contrast between the formalism of ritual observance and the reality of injustice.

61.1: +P
"Good news to the oppressed".

61.8: +J
"I, the Lord, love justice".

Summary

	S	-S	+S	P	-P	+P	J	-J	+J
Isaiah	7	7	0	15	0	15	20	2	18

1.4.2.   Jeremiah

Of all the prophets, Jeremiah is the one who leaves the deepest impression of his own person and circumstances. His story begins as the Kingdom of Judea is about to be over-run. Jeremiah's message that this is an inevitable consequence of wickedness such that the conquest of Judea should be welcomed and not avoided is deemed politically unacceptable, for which he is imprisoned. He goes on to tell of the collapse of Judea, the establishment of foreign rule, internecine strife, idolatry, and further collapse by the Judean remnant in Egypt. Not unnaturally, there is heart-searching about the causes of Judea's unfaithfulness, which is where we find Jeremiah's ethical concerns. In spite of his being a by-word for pessimism, there is much in the Book of Jeremiah which is ironic, and even funny.

5.1: +J
Jeremiah fears that it will not be possible to find a just person in the streets of Jerusalem.

5.4: +P
Jeremiah's somewhat ironic assumption that the rich will know better how to live rightly proves incorrect.

5.26–29: +P, +J
The Chosen People have become scoundrels, both unjust and oppressive of the poor.

6.13: +P
The universality of greed condemned.

7.5–10: +S, +P, +J
If the people repent of their injustice, oppression, and adultery they will be forgiven; not enough evidence to indicate whether "adultery" here means idolatry or a breach of marital fidelity; I have settled on the latter.

9.2: -S

"They are all adulterers . . . "; I take this to mean idolaters because it is too general to apply to adultery.

9.6: +P

Condemnation of "oppression upon oppression".

9.23: -P

The wealthy should not boast in their wealth. A useful, but marginal, precept.

13.22: -S

The Lord's justifiable revenge likened to 'justifiable' rape. There is no getting round the difficulty of this and similar passages.

22.3: +J, +P

Injunction to act with justice and protect the oppressed, including aliens.

22.13–17: +P

An ironic dig at the rich who build their ambitions on the backs of the poor; a good example of Jeremiah's sense of humour.

23.5: +J

The new ruler in the line of David will rule justly.

Summary

	S	-S	+S	P	-P	+P	J	-J	+J
Jeremiah	3	2	1	8	1	7	5	0	5

1.4.3. Lamentations

The Book of Lamentations, traditionally but incorrectly attributed to Jeremiah, is a profoundly beautiful and melancholy poem about the desolation of Jerusalem but, other than bemoaning idolatry, it does not go into the aetiology of the catastrophe. All scores are 0.

1.4.4. Ezekiel

Perhaps the most prophetic of the prophets, certainly the most other-worldly, Ezekiel's central concern is coming to terms with Judea's exile and the inevitable period of retribution and penitence.

16.49: -S
The sins of Sodom do not include homosexuality; cf. Genesis 13.13, 19.1–11.

18.5–9: +S, -S, +P, +J
A list of infractions including adultery, oppression and injustice.

20.5: +S, -S, +P, +J
Repeats 18.5–9.

22.6–12: +S, -S, +P, +J
Yet another list. The -S references in this book all refer to sexual intercourse during a woman's menstrual period; a matter of purity rather than sexual ethics.

22.29: +P
Part of Judea's woe is the result of extortion and oppression.

23: -S
The most extended and sexually explicit (v. 20) metaphor for idolatry clearly explained (v. 4).

33.26–27: +S
A list of serious offences, including adultery.

34.1–10: +P, +J
A remarkable piece of rhetoric against the false shepherds of the Chosen People.

34.17–22: +P
God will protect the weak and judge the wicked.

44.22: -S
On the marriage conditions for priests.

Summary

	S	-S	+S	P	-P	+P	J	-J	+J
Ezekiel	10	6	4	6	0	6	4	0	4

1.4.5. Daniel

The Book of Daniel is a mixture of apocalyptic statements and fascinating tales about Daniel during the exile, first under the Assyrians and then under the Persians. It was one of the most popular texts at the time of Jesus; not least because it points forward to a Messiah. In this context ethics are merely incidental.

4.27: +J
Stop sinning and be merciful to the poor.

5.2: -S
Wives and concubines are described without negative comment

5.23: -S
cf. 5.2.

Summary

	S	-S	+S	P	-P	+P	J	-J	+J
Daniel	2	2	0	0	0	0	1	0	1

1.4.6. Hosea

Hosea wrote just before the collapse of the Kingdom of Israel at the beginning of the sixth century BCE. Perhaps the most remarkable aspect of the Book of Hosea is not the author's elaborate sexual metaphor to represent Israel's idolatry, but the extent to which the metaphor has been ignored and the text interpreted literally.

1.2–3.5: -S
The sexual metaphor used to depict idolatry, clearly shown to be a metaphor at 2.13 onwards. It is only cited here because of its frequent misuse as a diatribe against adultery, rather than idolatry. The key point to bear in mind as part of our enquiry is that the number of Old Testament references thought relevant to sexual matters increases dramatically if metaphorical passages about idolatry are taken to be concerned with adultery.

4.2–3: +S, +P
A list of wrongdoing including adultery and stealing.

4.18: -S
Sexual orgies after drinking-bouts; could be actual or metaphorical.

7.4: -S
"They are all adulterers", i.e. idolaters.

12.6: +J
Hold fast to justice.

12.7: +P
Condemnation of economic oppression.

Summary

	S	-S	+S	P	-P	+P	J	-J	+J
Hosea	4	3	1	2	0	2	1	0	1

1.4.7. Joel

One of the most unremittingly severe of the prophets, Joel describes turmoil on the verge of Israel's collapse.

3.2–3: +S
Trade in children for wine and prostitutes; this may refer to slaves but it would not be so seriously condemned if it were the case. The conclusion must be that this is really depraved behaviour involving respectable people. Scored positive because of the contemporary concern with children being trafficked and sexually assaulted.

Summary

	S	-S	+S	P	-P	+P	J	-J	+J
Joel	1	0	1	0	0	0	0	0	0

1.4.8. Amos

Amos, apparently a shepherd, is deeply conscious of socio-economic injustice, and is the only prophet who cites this as one of the main causes of God's punishment of exile.

2.6–7: -S, +P
Against incest and oppression.

4.1: +P
Against the oppression of the poor.

5.12: +P
Against the oppression of the needy.

5.15: +J
Establish justice in the gate.

5.24: +J
Let justice roll down like waters.

6.4–6: +P
The fullest, most detailed and vivid attack on the luxury of the ruling classes.

8.4: +P
Condemnation of those who trample on the needy and ruin the poor.

Summary

	S	-S	+S	P	-P	+P	J	-J	+J
Amos	1	1	0	5	0	5	2	0	2

1.4.9. Micah

Micah is yet another prophet coming to terms with the imminent collapse of Judea and Israel.

1.7: -S

The gains of the people likened to the wages of a prostitute; a clear reference to idolatry.

2.2: +P

Covetousness and oppression condemned.

3.1: +J

" . . . Israel, should you not know justice?"

Summary

	S	-S	+S	P	-P	+P	J	-J	+J
Micha	1	1	0	1	0	1	1	0	1

1.4.10. Zechariah

Written during the reign of Darius of Persia, Zechariah is perhaps the most rewarding of the Minor Prophets.

5.7: -S

The woman in the basket representing wickedness.

7.8–10: +P, +J

In praise of justice and against the oppression of the poor and weak.

8.16: +J

A command to render justice.

14.2: -S

Another incident of women being raped as a divine instrument of punishment; cf. Jeremiah 13.22. Seen in its own terms, there may be a case for the Chosen People to believe that the Lord is instructing them to kill males capable of bearing arms as part of their military strategy. However, the rape of women seen as a divine instrument of the Lord's anger raises questions, not for the first time, about the misuse of non-combatants. On a wider level, we must begin to question the ethical value of any pronouncement in the Old Testament on the purposes and conduct of war.

Summary

	S	-S	+S	P	-P	+P	J	-J	+J
Zechariah	2	2	0	1	0	1	2	0	2

1.4.11. Malachi

3.5: -S, +P
The adultery reference looks like a reference to idolatry; the reference against the oppression of the poor is clear.

Summary

	S	-S	+S	P	-P	+P	J	-J	+J
Malachi	1	1	0	1	0	1	0	0	0

1.4.12. Minor Prophets

There are no references of interest to our enquiry in the Books of Obadiah, Jonah, Nahum, Habakkuk, Zephaniah, or Haggai, so all are scored at zero.

Conclusion

	S	-S	+S	P	-P	+P	J	-J	+J
Isiah	7	7	0	15	0	15	20	2	18
Jeremiah	3	2	1	8	1	7	5	0	5
Lamentations	0	0	0	0	0	0	0	0	0
Ezekiel	10	6	4	6	0	6	4	0	4
Daniel	2	2	0	0	0	0	1	0	1
Hosea	4	3	1	2	0	2	1	0	1
Joel	1	0	1	0	0	0	0	0	0
Amos	1	1	0	5	0	5	2	0	2
Obadiah	0	0	0	0	0	0	0	0	0
Jonah	0	0	0	0	0	0	0	0	0
Micah	1	1	0	1	0	1	1	0	1
Nahum	0	0	0	0	0	0	0	0	0
Habakkuk	0	0	0	0	0	0	0	0	0
Zephaniah	0	0	0	0	0	0	0	0	0
Haggai	0	0	0	0	0	0	0	0	0
Zechariah	2	2	0	1	0	1	2	0	2
Malachi	1	1	0	1	0	1	0	0	0
TOTAL	32	25	7	39	1	38	36	3	33

Although the number of references to each of our three topics are not all that far apart at 4 : 5 : 5, there is much greater variance between those which are scored as relevant to our enquiry, where the ratio is 1 : 5 : 4. It is also significant for our further discussions that the vast majority of relevant sexual references concern the virtues and comforts of marital fidelity and the condemnation of adultery. It is also significant that the highest scores for socio-economic and procedural justice are registered by Isaiah, the most cited prophet in the Gospels (see Chapter 2, p. 85).

1.5.   THE APOCRYPHA

The Apocryphal, or Deuterocanonical, books of the Bible are those which were added to the Septuagint, the Greek translation of the Hebrew Scriptures made in Alexandria, Egypt during the reign of Ptolemy II Adelphus in the middle of the Third Century BCE (although the first extant evidence for this is in the *Letter of Aristeas* some hundred years later). Thus, these books were never part of the initial Jewish Canon, but they were accepted by the united and divided Catholic Church for more than a thousand years. At the Reformation, a drive for textual authenticity marginalised these books, and certain sections of others, because they had not been part of what was seen as the 'authentic' Hebrew texts. Although they appeared in the King James Bible (Authorised Version, 1612), they gradually fell out of use so that only a very few passages, primarily from Ecclesiasticus, are read in church.

The books were, in general, written later than those in Section 1.4 (p. 52), between the end of the Jewish exile at the latter end of the sixth century BCE and the time of Jesus. They are largely either narrative or novel-like illustrations of heroism and faithfulness, and Greek influences are obvious not only in the narratives themselves but in the literary style. With the exceptions of The Wisdom of Solomon and Sirach (Ecclesiasticus), they are not much concerned with our issues. Many of the books have no citations of interest and will be scored as zero.

1.5.1.   Tobit

The Book of Tobit is a charming novella with lovingly drawn characters, dealing with the interwoven themes of righteousness, faithfulness, and the virtues and comforts of family life, with a very strange matrimonial twist.

1.3: +P
Approbation for Tobit's acts of charity.

1.16–17: +P
cf. 1.3.

2.1–6: +P
Tobias seeks out the poor.

4.7–10: +P
The importance of giving to the poor.

4.16: +P
Give your food to the poor.

8.17: +S
Against lust.

12.8–10: +P
It is better to give alms than store up gold.

14.7: +J
Injustice punished.

14.8–9: +P
cf. 12.8–190.

Summary

	S	-S	+S	P	-P	+P	J	-J	+J
Tobit	1	0	1	7	0	7	1	0	1

1.5.2. Judith

While there are no specific references in the Book of Judith to our three strands of enquiry, it is important to note in passing that this book is concerned with the use of feminine charm by Judith to achieve the assassination of Holofernes. As she emerged both victorious and sexually unscathed, the story has a kind of moral tidiness. However, this raises the question of whether the verdict would have been different if she had had to succumb sexually to Holofernes as part of the stratagem to murder him. On balance, I would answer in the affirmative, both because the survival of the Chosen People ranks above mere considerations of sexual conduct and because, in spite of the warm and complimentary portrait of Judith, she is still, after all, 'only' a woman.

1.5.3.   Greek Esther

I have commented on the Hebrew text of Esther in Section 1.2 (p. 29) and would only add that the book reads much better with the additions which appear only in the Septuagint.

1.5.4.   The Wisdom of Solomon

Like its Old Testament equivalents (see Section 1.3, p. 41), The Wisdom of Solomon is something of a rag-bag, although it has much more sustained passages, in the later literary style of the Apocryphal books.

1.6: +P
Wisdom is a kindly spirit.

2.1, 10–11: +P
Oppression is a matter of thinking unsoundly.

3.13: -S
It is better to be infertile than defiled.

3.15: -P
The fruit of good labour is renowned; marginally pragmatic rather than principled.

3.16–17: -S
Illegitimate children will not come to maturity but will perish. If they do not perish they will be of no account and will receive no honour in old age. A strange, contradictory passage, blaming the sins of parents on their children.

4.1: -S
Childlessness with virtue is better than its opposite.

4.3–6: -S
A colourful enlargement of 3.16–17.

6.1–8: +J
A divine insistence on justice.

8.7: +J
In praise of justice.

12.23: +P
The virtue of mercy.

Summary

	S	-S	+S	P	-P	+P	J	-J	+J
Wisdom of Solomon	4	4	0	4	1	3	2	0	2

1.5.5.   Sirach

The Book of Sirach, or Ecclesiasticus, is packed full of nostrums of varying value in the tradition of the Wisdom Books (see Section 1.3, p. 41), but is much more elaborate. Like the Book of Proverbs and the Book of Ecclesiastes (with which it should not be confused), there is a good deal of rhetorical posturing in Sirach which leads to citations being scored negatively, either for want of real moral force or because the sentiments are exaggerated. There is a high count of citations in this Book against female sexual misconduct; one wonders whether a person in a position of 'male headship' should not be held more responsible for their sexual conduct instead of blaming this on female seduction, particularly as there is a strong tendency to blame women for moral weakness! After some thought, I have scored the praise of good wives as minus because it is largely platitudinous and not balanced by any directives for the good husband.

2.11: +J
The Lord is compassionate and merciful; he forgives sins.

3.18: +P
The greater you are, the more you must humble yourself.

4.1–10: -P
Exhortations not to cheat the poor but largely pragmatic rather than ethical, so scored minus.

5.1: +P
Do not rely on wealth.

7.3: +J
Do not sow in the furrows of injustice.

7.10: +P
Do not neglect to give alms.

7.24: +S
Protect the chastity of daughters, scored positively because of the teaching, not because of the 'pastoral' stance of the Church of England.

7.27: +P
Against divorce, although slightly ambivalent, depending on how much the wife pleases the husband.

7.32: -P
Stretch out your hands to the poor; admirable but too weak to score positively.

8.2: -P
Gold has ruined the rich; pragmatic rather than moral.

9.1–9: +S
A colourful catalogue of women and situations to avoid; marginally positive.

11.12: +P
The eyes of the Lord are kind to those who need help.

14.9: +J
Without the soul, there is greedy injustice.

16.1–3: -S
Against ungodly offspring; it is better to be childless.

17.22: +P
Almsgiving is the apple of the Lord's eye.

17.29: +J
How great is the mercy of the Lord.

19.2: -S
Wine and women lead intelligent men astray!

22.3: -S
The birth of a daughter is a loss.

22.16: +S
Against lust, among other things, including fornication with kin.

23.17–21: +S
Against fornication by males; a highly unusual stricture.

23.22–27: +S
Against fornication and consequent adultery.

25.1: -S
In favour of matrimonial harmony

25.2: +S
Against "an old fool" who commits adultery.

25.8: -S
Happy the man with a good wife who does not commit adultery.

25.15: -S
No anger worse than a woman's!

25.16–26: -S
Against wicked women. It could be argued that most of the Biblical texts are implicitly descriptions of the shortcomings of men who are engaged as heads of families and in public life. The primary objection to passages such as this is that they assign wickedness to women because of their being women, whereas this does not happen to men.

26.1–9: -S
In favour of good wives and against bad wives; marginally scored negative.

26.10–12: -S
Against impudent daughters.

26.13–18: -S
In praise of good wives.

26.22–27: -S
Miscellaneous comments in favour of good, and against bad, women.

27.1: +P
Many have committed sin for gain.

29.1: +P
The merciful lend to their neighbours (interest free).

29.7–13: +P
Do not withhold alms.

31.1–10: +P
The dangers of riches; marginally scored positive after balancing principle and pragmatism.

34.25: +P
He who deprives the poor of bread is a murderer; a good example of exaggeration.

35.4: +P
Almsgiving.

35.17–20: +P
The Lord is merciful to orphans and widows, a matter of socio-economic rather than procedural mercy.

36.28–29: -S
In praise of good wives.

40.17: +P
Kindness is a garden of blessing.

40.19: -S
In praise of the blameless wife.

41.17: +P
Be ashamed of sexual immorality

41.20–22: +S, +P
Against depriving the needy, prostitution, and looking at another's wife.

42.9–14: -S
Against headstrong daughters.

Summary

	S	-S	+S	P	-P	+P	J	-J	+J
Sirach	21	14	7	19	3	16	4	0	4

1.5.6.　Baruch

Baruch, possibly Jeremiah's secretary (see Section 1.4, p. 52), tells of Judea's infidelity and exile.

3.18: +P
Condemns the wicked for love of silver.

Summary

	S	-S	+S	P	-P	+P	J	-J	+J
Baruch	0	0	0	1	0	1	0	0	0

1.5.7. 1 Esdras

Substantially the same as the Masoretic Ezra (see Section 1.2, p. 29).

4.13–32: -S
In a long, highly stylised discussion on the important things in life, Zerubbabel lists the uses and virtues of women, but also notes that they drive men to sin.

8.85: -S
Jewish men forbidden to marry foreign women, but no reciprocal pronouncement for women.

9.12–17: -S
The recurring theme of opposition to foreign wives.

Summary

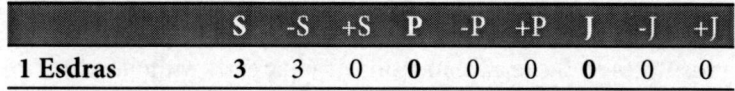

	S	-S	+S	P	-P	+P	J	-J	+J
1 Esdras	3	3	0	0	0	0	0	0	0

1.5.8.   2 Esdras

An apocalyptic work, attributed to Ezra (see Section 1.2, p. 29) whose only complete manuscript is in Latin.

2.22–24: +P
Care for the weak.

9.38–45: -S
The low estate of infertility.

14.13: -P
Comfort the lowly; not a strong enough indicator to score.

15.54–55: -S
The figure of the prostitute used to represent idolatry.

Summary

	S	-S	+S	P	-P	+P	J	-J	+J
2 Esdras	2	2	0	2	1	1	0	0	0

1.5.9.   The Letter of Jeremiah

Possibly the final chapter of Baruch.

6.11: -S
Prostitutes on the terrace mentioned apparently without criticism.

Summary

	S	-S	+S	P	-P	+P	J	-J	+J
Letter of Jeremiah	1	1	0	0	0	0	0	0	0

1.5.10. Susanna

The tale of Susanna is one of many pieces of the book of Daniel (see Section 1.4, p. 52), which only appears in the Septuagint. It is a tale against lust and in favour of justice.

1.1–15: +S
The description of the lust of the two judges for Susanna; an implicit condemnation.

Summary

	S	-S	+S	P	-P	+P	J	-J	+J
Susanna	1	0	1	0	0	0	0	0	0

1.5.11. 1 Maccabees

The Books of the Maccabees are largely concerned with heroic Judean resistance to externally imposed idolatry.

14.14: +P
Simon gave help to all the humble.

Summary

	S	-S	+S	P	-P	+P	J	-J	+J
1 Maccabees	0	0	0	1	0	1	0	0	0

1.5.12. 2 Maccabees

7: -S
The remarkable heroism of a widow who urges her seven sons to be tortured to death rather than eat pork. The story is vivid and puts the widow in a good light; particularly interesting considering the usual view of widows which, in this case, might read: " . . . even widows can resist idolatry and so everybody should be able to do so".

Summary

	S	-S	+S	P	-P	+P	J	-J	+J
2 Maccabees	1	1	0	0	0	0	0	0	0

1.5.13. 4 Maccabees

4 Maccabees has a self-conscious, philosophical approach.

2.1–6: +S
Urges the rational control of sexual desire.

2.6–9: +P
Reason points towards social justice.

2.10: -S
Reason superior to love of a wife.

5.24: +J
The Law teaches justice.

8–12: -S
The unlikely widow Ahain; cf. 2 Maccabees 7.

14.11–17.16: -S
In praise of the courage of women; quite remarkable given all that
has gone before.

18.16–24: -S
The victorious mother.

Summary

	S	-S	+S	P	-P	+P	J	-J	+J
4 Maccabees	5	4	1	1	0	1	1	0	1

1.5.14. Other Books

There are no relevant references to our topics in Judith, the (Greek)
additions to Esther, the Prayer of Azariah, and the Song of the
Three Jews, Bel and the Dragon, 3 Maccabees, or the Prayer of
Manasseh.

Conclusion

	S	-S	+S	P	-P	+P	J	-J	+J
Tobit	1	0	1	7	0	7	1	0	1
Wisdom of Solomon	4	4	0	4	1	3	2	0	2
Sirach	21	14	7	19	3	16	4	0	4

	S	-S	+S	P	-P	+P	J	-J	+J
Baruch	0	0	0	1	0	1	0	0	0
1 Esdras	3	3	0	0	0	0	0	0	0
2 Esdras	2	2	0	2	1	1	0	0	0
Letter of Jeremiah	1	1	0	0	0	0	0	0	0
Song of Three Jews	0	0	0	0	0	0	0	0	0
Susanna	1	0	1	0	0	0	0	0	0
Bel and the Dragon	0	0	0	0	0	0	0	0	0
1 Maccabees	0	0	0	1	0	1	0	0	0
2 Maccabees	1	1	0	0	0	0	0	0	0
3 Maccabees	0	0	0	0	0	0	0	0	0
4 Maccabees	5	4	1	1	0	1	1	0	1
Manasseh	0	0	0	0	0	0	0	0	0
TOTAL	39	29	10	35	5	30	8	0	8

The number of citations is slightly different from the Old Testament at 5 : 4 : 1 with a markedly low score for procedural justice. However, when we look at the relevant citations, the ratio of roughly 1 : 3 : 1 shows a steady score for relevant citations on power and wealth.

1.6. THE OLD TESTAMENT RECKONING

	S	-S	+S	P	-P	+P	J	-J	+J
Pentatuch	61	46	15	25	3	22	9	1	8
Narratives	47	45	2	4	0	4	1	0	1
Wisdom	54	15	9	43	7	36	15	2	13
Prophets	32	25	7	39	1	38	36	3	33

	S	-S	+S	P	-P	+P	J	-J	+J
TOTAL	**164**	131	33	**111**	11	100	**61**	6	55

As we would probably expect, by far the largest number of references are to our first category of sex and gender, but approximately four fifths of these are not relevant to our enquiry and many of them are simply cultural misogyny. Of the thirty-three that remain, the vast majority either support marital fidelity or condemn adultery, but the context seems to be much more concerned with property rights than sexual ethics *per se*. The issue of how we view the Old Testament attitude to adultery will be a core consideration in subsequent discussions.

By contrast, there are very few of the 111 references to power and wealth that are not relevant. Thus, although the number of citations for this category is approximately three fifths of those concerning sex and gender, the relevant references in this category out-score the first by 3 : 1.

The third category has been included as a kind of bench mark against which to judge the first two but, even here, its relevant references are approaching twice as many as those for the first category.

Even before we reach the New Testament, then, it is clear that the citations on issues of socio-economic and procedural justice, as they apply to us today, far outweigh the citations on sex and gender.

For the completionists, of which I am one, here is the Old Testament and Apocrypha added together:

	S	-S	+S	P	-P	+P	J	-J	+J
Old Testament	**164**	131	33	**111**	11	100	**61**	6	55
Apocrypha	**39**	29	10	**35**	5	30	**8**	0	8
TOTAL	**202**	160	43	**146**	16	130	**69**	6	63

2.   THE NEW TESTAMENT

The Christian New Testament consists of all those works which came, at the beginning of the fifth century CE, to be accepted by the Church as canonical. There are still many unsettled questions about authorship which, for example, make it difficult to divide letters written and probably not written by Paul. As this is not the place for that debate, I have chosen to divide the New Testament as follows:

- The Gospels (Section 2.1)
- Acts (Section 2.2)
- Letters (Section 2.3)
- The Book of Revelation (Section 2.4).

Although it should not be necessary, I need to make a comment on the way I have scored the concept of "love" in the Gospel of John, in Paul, and in the later letter writers (see Section 2.3, p. 115). Taking the Gospels and letters at their word, and following in a tradition of almost 2000 years which has survived any amount of bossiness and moralising, I take the highest Christian value to be that of love. Where this term occurs, then, I have usually scored it as plus in each of the three categories, assuming that it should encompass loving sexual activity and loving orientation towards gender roles, a constructive attitude to socio-economic justice and an acceptance of the highest possible standard of procedural justice. The word 'love' is also used of the relationship between Jesus and 'The Father' and the love of Jesus for humanity, but this is not relevant to our concerns and is not scored at all.

2.1.   THE GOSPELS

The Gospels tell the story of Jesus who lived for approximately 33 years between 6 BCE and 33 CE. They were written between 60 and 110 CE, the earliest being Mark, followed by Matthew, Luke, and John. To a large extent, the dating of these texts depends upon the assumption that the destruction of the Temple in 70 CE was reported rather than anticipated in the Gospels, but recently Richard Bauckham has made a strong case for earlier authorship.[4] Those in favour of earlier dating tend to be more affirmative in their belief that the Gospels report direct speech, while those who support later dating tend to see the Gospels as theological redactions by their authors.

In spite of extensive research it has proved fruitless to try to identify how authentic these accounts are, particularly in relation to the reported speech of Jesus. That Jesus lived, conducted a ministry of one to three years, and was 'tried' and crucified has been established beyond reasonable doubt. Likewise, there was no doubt among his followers and the Gospel writers that Jesus, in some way, rose from the dead three days after his entombment.

In considering the Gospels I have, as with the Old Testament and Apocrypha, taken the authors at their word so that all parts of the Bible are taken to be the Word of God, although this does not rule out pertinent commentary.

2.1.1.   Matthew

Although it has now been almost universally accepted that the ancient authorities were wrong in placing Matthew's Gospel before Mark, I have retained the traditional ordering.

Eusebius (d. 341) records that Papias, a bishop in Asia Minor in the early second century, said that the Apostle Matthew wrote an

---

4   Richard Bauckham, *Jesus and The Eyewitnesses: The Gospels as EyeWitness Testimony* (Eerdmans, 2008).

account of the sayings of Jesus in Hebrew, based on the tradition that the author was the Matthew of 9.9. However, the manuscript ascribed to Matthew appears to have been an original Greek text. The consensus, in spite of Bauckham, is that it was written between 70–90 CE. It certainly shows evidence of the Judaeo-Christian friction which grew as the first century CE progressed, and therefore it can hardly have been written before Christians self-consciously differentiated themselves from Jews.

1.1–17: -S

The genealogy contains references to women as well as non-Jews and morally questionable characters.

1.18–25: -S

cf. Isaiah 7.14. Matthew is referring to the Septuagint Greek *parthenos* as a translation of the Hebrew *Almah* in Isaiah 7.14, which is usually taken to mean 'young woman'. The technical Hebrew term for virgin is *betulah* which is used more than fifty times in the Tanakh, including several times in Isaiah. The significance here is not the theological doctrine but the history of Christianity and gender: the doctrine of the virgin birth did not emerge until the middle of the second century CE, coinciding with a rise in Gnosticism which Christianity supposed itself to oppose. It is very difficult to deny a progressively misogynistic early Christian Church, almost from the death of Jesus.

3.4: +P

John's coarse clothing and spare diet as marks of discipleship.

3.8: +P

"Bear fruit worthy of repentance" indicates that mere words are not good enough; they require good deeds to accompany them.

1.19: +S

" . . . Minded to put her away", i.e., against fornication.

4.8–10: +P
The third temptation of worldly power rejected by Jesus.

4.18–22: +P
Peter, Andrew, James, and John apparently renounce their earthly possessions to follow Jesus. The implication is only marginally strong enough to merit a plus.

5.3: -P
"Blessed are the poor in spirit" may refer to Isaiah 6.1–3 but, on balance, the meaning is closer to 'humility' than poverty.

5.5: +P
The meek will inherit the earth implies that the proud will not, and that it is worth inheriting (I recall with pleasure Eric Morecambe's quip that the meek will inherit the earth because they will not have the nerve to refuse it!). On balance, a positive score.

5.7: +J
The merciful will receive mercy; apparently pragmatic but, given its position, scores positive.

5.8: -S
"Blessed are the pure in heat"; often assumed to refer to the evils of adultery but there is no evidence for this.

5.27–30: +S
Not only against adultery but also against vicarious lust.

5.31–32: +S
Against divorce; cf. Deuteronomy 24.1–4. Jesus is even stricter than Deuteronomy: "Whoever marries a divorced woman commits adultery". This statement is underscored because of its relevance to subsequent discussion.

5.38–41: +J
Ranks mercy above pure, procedural justice.

5.42: +P
Give to those who ask.

5.43–48: +P, +J
Ranks love above ordinary dealing; cf. Leviticus 19.18–19.

6.2: +P
Giving alms; cf. Deuteronomy 14.28–29, 15.11, 19.24.

<u>6.10: +S, +P, +J</u>
"Your will be done, on earth as it is in heaven". I take this to apply to all our three categories.

<u>6.12, 14–15: +J</u>
Forgive.

6.19–21: +P
"Do not store up for yourselves treasure on earth" has a strongly pragmatic feeling but I marginally score it positive.

6.24–34: +P
The strong implication is that serving wealth rules out serving God; there is also a powerful warning against accumulation of wealth. The ideal of the lilies of the field is almost impossible to follow in view of prudential obligations to family but the citation does not instruct us either to be idle or fatalistic.

7.1: -J
"Do not judge, so that you may not be judged". This is clearly not a citation against procedural justice as perceived in the Torah, but seems more to refer to assigning moral or social judgments on top of procedural judgments. The Torah is far from being mechanistic— this is a Christian caricature. However, Christianity does tend to

emphasise motive rather than outcome, and we never can know the circumstances in which other people make ethical decisions, even if they narrate the circumstances from their own perspective. For the purposes of this enquiry, the important point is whether the Church has any procedural role, outside the confessional, which entitles it to judge individual behaviour in general and sexual behaviour in particular.

7.13–14: +P
Wealth is an obstacle to salvation; apparently pragmatic but I give it a marginal plus.

9.9: -P
It may be that Matthew gave up everything to follow Jesus but the indication is not strong enough for a plus.

9.13: +J
Jesus wants Pharisees to be merciful rather than demanding sacrifices of reparation from sinners.

10.9–13: +P
Those who spread the word of Jesus must carry the minimum; it might be unfair to apply this specifically to clergy.

10.17–42: +P
The first great statement about suffering as part of discipleship.

11.5: +P
"The poor have good news brought to them." In one respect, all have good news brought to them but there does seem to be a particular emphasis here on the weak and the poor, and this at least implies a greater measure of socio economic justice.

11.23: -S, +P
Deeds of power are worse than the deed of Sodom, whatever that is; cf. Genesis 19.4–11.

11.28–30: +P
"My yoke is easy . . . " This could refer to spiritual matters but I marginally score it to include the socio-economic.

12.39: -S
As Jesus uses the term "adulterous generation" in response to a request for a miraculous sign, the reference is to idolatry.

13.7–22: +P
The seed fallen in the thorns representing worldliness.

14.3–4: -S
John told Herod that he could not marry his brother Philip's wife.

15.19: +S
Inclusion of adultery and fornication in a list of wrong-doing.

16.24–26: +P
Following Jesus involves self-denial.

16.26: +P
The whole world is not equal in value to one's (spiritual) life.

18.21–22: +J
The importance of forgiveness compared with procedural justice.

18.23–35: +J
cf. 6.12, 14–15.

19.3–9: +S
cf. Genesis 1.27, Deuteronomy 24.1–4. Deuteronomy allows a husband to divorce a wife for "unchastity" but not vice versa. However, by the time of Jesus, the introduction of Roman law meant that women had begun to institute divorce proceedings. Rabbinic opinion varied from the House of Shammai, which is very close to that of Jesus' interpretation of marriage as being anchored

in the creation narrative, to the more lenient House of Hillel. . The dividing issue was the level of (female) infraction that could trigger a divorce. The more lenient interpretation might allow divorce for less serious issues, and there is a hint that mere male dissatisfaction with a wife might be grounds for divorce (cf. Sirach 7.27). . This raises the possibility that Jesus' strictness on the matter might have been motivated by a desire to protect wives against arbitrary husbands. There is a plausible argument that the more financially secure the wife and/or children, the less justification there is for shoring up failed marriages; i.e., divorce for marital breakdown is more acceptable if women can maintain themselves and/or their children in a separate household. The question might have been raised in the context of some of the followers of Jesus contemplating leaving their wives to lead celibate, itinerant lives.

19.18–20: +S, +P, +J
cf. Leviticus 19.18.

19.20–26: +P
The eye of a needle: an exacting price of discipleship. A somewhat pragmatic observation which I have scored positive but this is balanced by my negative scoring of the next citation.

19.27–29: -P
Although there is a long Christian tradition of contractual ethical compliance, caricatured in the Reformation argument against Catholic "Good works", we should be suspicious of the argument, recalling Edward Caswell's translation of the Spanish sonnet to the crucified Christ: "My God, I love thee not because I hope for heaven thereby". hope for heaven thereby".[5] Marked negative to balance the previous marginal citation.

---

[5] "No me mueve, mi Dios, para quererte / el cielo que me tienes prometido", Anon., *Soneta a Cristo crucificado*, 1–2.

19.30: +P
Those first in earthly power will be last into paradise. Somewhat pragmatic but scores positive on balance.

20.1–16: -P
Although this is a parable about entrance into the Kingdom of Heaven it nicely summarises the principle of equal entitlement versus piecework payment.

20.20–23: -P
Does not refer to the exercise of earthly power.

20.25–27: +P
Service as part of discipleship.

21.12–13: -P
A rather strange condemnation, unless Jesus is condemning the practice of changing foreign currency into the high quality Tyrian Shekel, which is the only currency the Temple authorities would accept; cf. Isaiah 56.7, Jeremiah 7.11. A hard interpretation would be that worship and trade are incompatible.

21.32: -S
A good word for tax collectors and prostitutes.

22.1–14: -P
Much less egalitarian than Luke 14.15–24.

22.15–22: -P
At the time of Jesus, taxation had no redistributive function and so there is no indication for a positive score. Incidentally, verse 21 is often taken to mean that Jesus supported the payment of taxes to the Romans. However, the verse is also, perhaps deliberately, open to the interpretation that if everything belongs to God, nothing should be paid to the Romans.

22.23–33: -S
cf. Genesis 38.8–20, Deuteronomy 25.5–20; apparently a trick question on the complexities in heaven of Levirate marriage, but actually a trick question to discredit the notion of bodily resurrection.

22.39: +S, +P, +J
cf. 19.18–20, confirms the score in all three categories.

23.1–5: -P
There is just a hint that the Pharisees are imposing on the poor, but not strong enough to merit a positive score.

23.23: +J
Justice and mercy are more important than the legalism of tithes.

25.14–30: -P
cf. Luke 19.11–27. This story of the talents is (apparently correctly) taken to be a parable about righteousness but, in view of Torah (cf. Deuteronomy 23.19) and later Christian strictures on usury, the eye watering interest rate of 100% leaves me sympathising with the chastised slave!

25.31–46: +P
A very strong injunction to social justice and compassion, reinforced by repetition. A problem text for classical Lutherans and some other reformed congregations. It has a pragmatic element but still scores positive.

26.6–13: -P
Jesus' stance against the anger of his apostles that we always have the poor with us has been used in Christian tradition to justify indifference to the poor; the response of Jesus is also just a little arch.

Summary

	S	-S	+S	P	-P	+P	J	-J	+J
Matthew	16	8	8	37	11	26	12	1	11

The initial impression is that there is a strong cluster of teachings in the Sermon on the Mount (Chapters 5–7) on socio-economic issues counterbalanced by a good smattering of sexual references which are, as usual, mostly concerned with adultery. But a closer examination shows references to wealth, power, and procedural justice distributed throughout the text, and although the majority of sexual references are to adultery and divorce, the forcefulness of Jesus' teaching on the issue cannot be easily overlooked.

The ratio of relevant references to our three topics is striking, with socio-economic justice scoring 3: 1 compared with sex and gender issues. Even our benchmark issue of procedural justice fares slightly better on relevant citations than sex and gender.

2.1.2. Mark

The earliest manuscripts attest a gospel "according to Mark", but it is likely that headings were added at a later date than composition to give the texts authority. It is possible that Mark is the same person mentioned elsewhere in the New Testament: cf. Acts 12.12, 15.37; Colossians 4.10; 2 Timothy 4.11; Philemon 24; and 1 Peter 5.13. Papias (see the introduction to Matthew, Section 2.1.1, p. 86), believed that Mark had accompanied Peter to Rome and recorded what Peter said, although he considered this less reliable than Matthew who was supposed to be an original follower. As the earliest of the Gospels, it was probably written in part around the time of the destruction of the Temple in 70 CE although corroborating references are vague (cf. 13.2, 7, 14–17). The most likely location for authorship is Antioch. Mark's terse literary style has often been conflated with simplicity, but twentieth-century developments in film, television, and deftly edited media have raised its reputation because there is a consonance between the techniques in this first gospel and contemporary sensibility

1.6: +P
cf. Matthew 3.4. John's simple attire and diet a pointer to discipleship.

1.16–20: +P
cf. Matthew 4.18–22 in identical language; the implication is only just worthy of a plus.

2.13–14: -P
cf. Matthew 9.9.

4.7, 18–19: +P
cf. Matthew 13.7, 22.

5.25–34: -P
cf. Matthew 9.20–22. An uncharacteristically lengthy account compared with Matthew, which mentions the woman's poverty, but all the evidence points to her being healed because of her faith, not her poverty.

6.8–11: +P
cf. Matthew 10.9–13.

6.17–18: -S
cf. Matthew 14.3–4.

7.21–22: +S, +P
cf. Matthew 15.19. Mark's list is fuller than Matthew's, and contains avarice and envy as well as sexual wrongdoing.

8.34–38: +P
cf. Matthew 10.17–42, 16.24.

8.36: +P
cf. Matthew 146.26.

8.38: -S
cf. Matthew 12.39.

<u>10.2–13: +S</u>
cf. Matthew 5.31–32.

10.17–27: +P
cf. Matthew 19.20–26.

10.31: +P
cf. Matthew 19.30.

10.35–40: -P
cf. Matthew 20.20–23, where it is the mother of the James and John who does the pleading.

10.42: +P
cf Matthew 20.25–27.

11.15–17: -P
cf. Matthew 21.12–13.

11.25: +J
cf. Matthew 18.21–22.

12.13–17: -P
cf. Matthew 22.15–22.

12.18–27: -S
cf. Matthew 22.23–33.

<u>12.31–33: +S, +P, +J</u>
cf. Matthew 19.18–20.

12.40: +P
cf. Matthew 23.1–6. It is difficult to imagine the religious authorities breaking down the houses of widows but the metaphor is somewhat obscure. Consequently, this reference alone would score negative, but the whole passage contrasting the rich and the poor scores positive.

12.41–44: +P
The implication of the "widow's mite" is that generosity is essential.

14.3–9: -P
cf. Matthew 26.6–13.

Summary

	S	-S	+S	P	-P	+P	J	-J	+J
Mark	6	3	3	19	6	13	2	0	2

The number of relevant sex and gender references is very low, which accounts for an even greater ratio in favour of socio-economic justice, at 4 : 1, compared with Matthew. Our benchmark of procedural justice is not far behind sex and gender on relevant references, though both numbers are very small.

2.1.3. Luke

The Gospel of Luke, together with the Acts of the Apostles (Luke/Acts) is traditionally ascribed to the physician Luke who was supposed to be Saint Paul's travelling companion; cf. Colossians 4.14, 2 Timothy 4.11, Philemon 1.24. Luke was not, and did not claim to be, an eyewitness (1.2), but sought to elaborate and correct earlier sources (1.1–4) which included parts of Mark (but not 6.45–8.26 nor 9.41–10.12), a source text referred to as Q, and also the author's own material (L). Luke is traditionally grouped with

Matthew and Mark as a "Synoptic" Gospel, but certain aspects of its tone and content display some commonality with John; or, perhaps it might be better to say that John has some consonance with Luke. The first two chapters emphasise continuity with the Hebrew Scriptures. A significant proportion of the text is taken up by the insertion of the travel narrative (cf. 9.51–18.14) into a Marcan structure, and Luke has a particularly vivid store of his own parables. Luke also has unique accounts of the Nativity of Jesus, and his childhood, Resurrection, and Ascension. In spite of his introductory avowal (cf. 1.1–4), Luke is not always accurate even in terms of the material at his disposal. He was almost certainly a Gentile writing primarily for Gentiles sometime between 70–100 CE, although Bauckham (see the introduction to The Gospels, Section 2.1, p. 86) and his followers would support an earlier date, and some scholars believe that the first two chapters were written much later in response to Marcion.

Luke has traditionally been seen as displaying particular concern with 'marginalised' people such as women, children, the sick, and the poor, but I am persuaded by Levin *et al* .when they say that

> This configuration begs the question, "marginal to what?" Luke's Gospel instead reveals that Jewish women had freedom of travel (1.39; 8.2–3; 23.27, 55–56) and access to their own funds (7.37; 8.3; 15.8; 21.2); undertook patronage roles (8.1–3); owned homes (10.38; see also Acts 12.12); and appeared in synagogues (13.10.17) and the Temple (2.22, 36–37, 41–50) . . . Most people in antiquity were poor, and the Jewish system, starting with the Tanakh, mandated communal responsibility for their care. To regard Jesus, appropriately, as caring for women, children, the sick and the poor embeds him within Judaism rather than separates him from it.[6]

---

[6]   Amy-Jill Levine and Marc Zvi Brettler (eds), *The Jewish Annotated New Testament (NRSV)* (Oxford University Press, 2011), p. 96.

1–7: -S
Elizabeth was barren, suffering socio-economic misfortune, anticipating an angelic intervention, and the conception of a special son; cf. Genesis 11.30; Judges 13.2–3, etc.

1.24–25: -S
Elizabeth's disgrace removed.

1.27: -S
The Virgin Mary; cf. Matthew 1.18–25 notes.

1.35: -S
The virginal conception; cf. Matthew 1.18–25 notes.

1.46–55: +P
The Magnificat; cf. 1 Samuel 2.1–10. In its directness, e.g., "brought down the powerful from their thrones . . . and sent the rich away empty", this is the most powerful passage of advocacy for socio-economic justice in the whole of the Bible. The prayer is said or sung every day in churches and cathedrals of the Anglican Communion where the service of Evensong is celebrated, without much apparent socioeconomic impact!

1.77–78: +J
Salvation through the merciful forgiveness of sins.

2.7: +P
Whether or not Jesus was born in a stable (the likelihood is that wherever he was born he was laid in a feeding trough in the animal part, i.e., the ground floor of an inn or *Kataluma*), he was certainly not born rich and this takes on immense symbolic significance.

2.8: -P
It is widely believed that the significance of shepherds is that they, outcasts and/or ritually impure, were the first to hear the good news of the birth of Jesus which, in turn, underlies Jesus'

fundamentally socio-economic message. However, this is incorrect, as shepherds were neither outcast nor impure. The significance is rather generative and dynastic, as Abel was the first shepherd and Moses was a shepherd, as were the Patriarchs, Abraham, Isaac, and Jacob. King David, the greatest of only three kings of the unified Judea and Israel, was a Bethlehem shepherd and the most illustrious progenitor of the hereditary line expected to produce the Messiah; cf. e.g. Genesis 4.1–2, 12.16, 30.31–32; Exodus 3.1; 1 Samuel 16.11–12.

2.36: -S
The female prophet Anna is one of many females paired with a male figure in Luke.

3.10–11: +P
John calls for food sharing and donating surpluses.

3.12–13: +P, +J
Tax collectors must be fair.

3.14: +P, +J
Soldiers must not extort and must be content with their wages.

3.18–20: -S
The imprisonment of John the Baptist for protesting Herod's marriage to his brother Philip's wife; cf. Matthew 14.3–4.

4.5–8: +P
Jesus' rejection of the temptation of worldly power; cf. Matthew 4.8–10.

<u>4.18–19: +P</u>
Jesus citing Isaiah 61.1–2 (Luke omits "the day of vengeance" in 61.2); cf. 58.6. The citation is underlined because this synagogue scene is often described as the Gospel's 'signature story'.

5.11: +P
His followers left all and followed Jesus; cf. Matthew 4.18–22.

5.27–28: +P
The tax collector Levi (Matthew) gives up everything to follow Jesus; a much stronger reference than Matthew 9.9.

6.20: +P
The beginning of Luke's "Sermon on the plain"; I score the references positive because, by inference, we should follow the teaching of Jesus. The poor are blessed for theirs is the kingdom of God; a much more direct reference than Matthew's "poor in spirit"; cf. Matthew 5.3.

6.21: +P
The hungry will be filled; again much stronger than Matthew 5.6 where the hunger is not physical but "after righteousness".

6.22: +P
Among others blessed are the excluded.

6.24: +P
Woe to the rich.

6.25: +P
Woe to the full.

6.29: -P
This is a response to criminal activity, not an exhortation to generosity.

6.30: -P
Half of the citation is generous, the other a response to criminal activity, making it, on balance, negative.

6.31: +S, +P, +J
The golden rule; cf. Leviticus 19.18, Matthew 19.18–20.

6.35: +P
Lend but expect nothing in return.

6.36: +J
Be merciful.

6.37: -J
A reference to moral judgment, not procedural justice.

6.38: +P
Give.

6.45: +P
There is a strong implication that badness is equated with treasure.

7.11–15: -S
The revival of the son of the widow of Nain reflects the archetypical view of widows.

7.20–22: +P
Among other benefits of Jesus, the poor receive good news. This can hardly simply be that the poor hear from Jesus what everybody else hears, i.e., it is not just a lack of exclusion.

7.29: -J
"The justice of God" is separate from procedural justice.

7.37–39: -S
It is frequently assumed, without any evidence whatsoever, that the woman in question is a sexual sinner although there is no hint of this in Matthew 26.6–13 or Mark 14.3–9. It is highly unlikely that a prostitute would possess so much money, though a mistress might. The passage is frequently associated, perhaps because of its

proximity to 8.2, with Mary Magdalen who, in turn, is assumed without evidence to be a sexual sinner.. Loosened hair is a sign, among other things, of grief or propitiation, and is not necessarily, nor even primarily, erotic.

8.7: +P
, 14: The thorns that choke the Word of God; cf. Matthew 13.7, 22; Mark 4.7, 18–19.

8.43, 48: -P
The woman cured because of her faith not her poverty, cf. Mark 25, 34.

9.1–5: +P
The sending out with the minimum necessities; cf. Matthew 14.12–14.

9.23–27: +P
Followers must deny themselves; cf. Matthew 10.17–42, 16.24.

9.48: +P
"The least among you is the greatest"; cf. Matthew 18.1–5.

10.4–11: +P
cf. 9.1–5.

10.12–15: -S, +P
cf. Matthew 11.23.

<u>10.25–37: +P</u>
The parable of the Good Samaritan describes an act of generosity by a Samaritan to a Jew; cf. 2 Chronicles 28.8–15. Incidentally, contrary to some interpretations, ritual purity is not an issue here. The injunction to do likewise could not be stronger, which justifies the underlining.

11.4: +J
cf. Matthew 23.23.

11.45: +P, +J
Against the burdens of lawyers; cf. Matthew 23.4.

12.15–21: +P
A parable against greed, the danger of possessions and the uncertainty of the time of death has a pragmatic element but is largely moralistic.

12.22–31: +P
cf. Matthew 6.24–34.

12.32–34: +P
Another call to poverty.

12.58: +J
Moral self-judgment is better than procedural justice.

13.6–9: +J
The parable of the infertile fig tree, given another chance.

14.7–11: -P
The parable of the banqueting table scores minus because, although it may have a background moral purpose, it is primarily pragmatic.

4.12–14: +P
The parable of the banqueting guests.

14.15–24: +P
The parable of the absent guests and their replacement relates poverty and weakness to entering the Kingdom.

15.30: +S
Against the use of prostitutes.

16.13: +P
"You cannot serve God and wealth" preceded by an equivocal parable of the dishonest steward; cf. Matthew 6.24.

16.14: +P
"Pharisee", a term of opprobrium in Luke, is caricatured as a lover of money, but the message holds.

18.18: +S
Against divorce but confined to one verse; cf. Matthew 19.9.

16.19–31: +P
The parable of the rich man (Dives) and Lazarus. There are times when Luke has something of a Pelagian turn!

17.3–4: +J
On forgiveness; cf. Matthew 18.15, 21–22.

18.1–9: -J
The parable of the goaded judge unfavourably compares procedural with divine justice.

18.9–14: +P
The parable of the Pharisee and the tax collector is primarily about humility and exaltation but it has a substantial power element.

18.18–20: +S
A list of wrong doing including adultery; cf. Matthew 19.18.

18.22–25: +P
The eye of a needle; cf. Matthew 19.20–24.

19.1–10: +P
Zacchaeus makes restitution for his wrongs; cf. Exodus 21.1.

19.11–27: -P
cf. Matthew 25.14–30, even more incongruous in the Lucan context!

19.45–46: -P
cf. Matthew 21–12–13.

20.20–26: -P
cf. Matthew 22.15–22.

20.27–39: -S
cf. Matthew 22.23–33.

20.45–47: +P
cf. Matthew 23.1–6.

21.1–4: +P
cf. Mark 12.41–44.

21.34–36: -P
Primarily pragmatic; scores minus.

23.34: +J
Jesus forgives his persecutors.

23.39–43: +J
The repentant thief granted ultimate forgiveness.

Summary

	S	-S	+S	P	-P	+P	J	-J	+J
Luke	14	10	4	49	9	40	15	3	12

As we would expect from Luke's reputation, his concern with socio-economic justice is paramount and scores much higher than our other two sets of citations put together.

2.1.4. John

Unlike the other three Gospels, the Gospel of John is clear that Jesus, in the incarnate Word made flesh, is the Son of God. It presents a glorious eschatological salvation which is also somehow present.

Eusebius cites Clement of Alexandria (c. 150–211/16) as saying that this fourth Gospel was written last to supplement the other three, but, although John repeats some incidents from the earlier Gospels, there is no evidence that he had access to a complete manuscript of any of them. Its 'high Christology' has led to many believing that it was written at the end of the first century CE (although cf. Philippians 2.6–11, written before 70 CE) but the most persuasive evidence is the Rylands Library Papyrus 52 of a tiny fragment of John 18.31–33, 37–38 from c.135/160 CE which would have taken some decades to arrive in Egypt from Asia Minor, pointing towards a composition date c.90 CE. It appears that the work is not from a single hand: there are narrative inconsistencies and sudden shifts (cf. 14.31); the story of the woman taken in adultery (cf. 7.53–8.13) was not from John at all and properly follows Luke 21.38; and the last Chapter looks suspiciously like a much later addition. The Gospel is traditionally supposed to have been written by the "Beloved Disciple" (cf. 13.23), and at an early stage this figure was conflated with John, son of Zebedee (again, Richard Bauckham has a fascinating, alternative perspective).[7] The purpose of the Gospel is set out in its original final verses (cf. 20.30.31), but the phrase "so that you may come to believe" is better translated from some manuscripts as "so that you may continue to believe", which better suits the text as a whole. The Gospel appears

---

[7]   Bauckham, op. cit.

to have been written for a mixed audience and is the most eclectic in its influences.

2.14–16: -P
There seems to be no anti-commercial sentiment; cf. Matthew 21.12–13.

3.17: +J
God did not send his son to condemn, so why should we?

4.5–30: -S
The story of the Samaritan woman who has had "five husbands" (17–18), viewed through contemporary experience, appears to be a woman who, to use contemporary language, is severely intellectually challenged and who has been exploited by at least six men whom Jesus tactfully refers to as "husbands". Jesus does not chide the woman and so I do not take this to be a positive score against adultery or fornication. A woman drawing water in the middle of the day is either 'simple', outcast, or both.

5.24–38: -J
On divine judgment.

7.53–8.13: +S
The woman is accused of adultery, a charge which she does not deny; the implication of Jesus being that we are all sinners. He refuses to condemn her and tells her not to sin again; scores positive. The passage has been detached from Luke and attached to John.

8.12–20: -J
On divine judgment.

10.11, 15, 17–18: +P
"The good shepherd lays down his life for the sheep"; another instance of the cost of discipleship from which an inference of compassion is legitimate.

12.1–8: -S, +P
cf. Matthew 26.6–13; in this version of the story we learn that the followers of Jesus kept money specifically to be donated to the poor. As Mary is anointing, there are no erotic overtones here!

13.1: +S, +P, +J
The only issue in doubt concerning Jesus' love is whether it is confined to "his own". I take the view that this is universal not particular.

13.12–17: +P
The nature of service is humility. This might only apply to religious leaders but I take it to apply to all followers of Jesus.

13.29: +P
There is a presumption that the store of money may be used either for necessities or to give to the poor.

13.34–35: +S, +P, +J
cf. 13.12–17; love.

14.15: +S, +P, -J
As there is a specific reference to the Commandments, the injunction can only apply to matters specified in them. The Torah is very generous in matters of socio-economic justice and specific about procedural justice, but the concern of the Commandments is restricted.

14.23–24: +S, +P, +J
Jesus' word is much broader than the Commandments.

15.12–15: +S, +P, +J
cf. 13.12–17; love.

21.15–17: -P
I take this to be a spiritual not a physical direction.

Summary

	S	-S	+S	P	-P	+P	J	-J	+J
John	8	2	6	11	3	8	8	3	5

Of all the evangelists, John is the least concerned with our subjects and his various uses of the word "love" makes scoring difficult. Thus, even though I do not think that the references to "love" that I have scored are very strongly linked with our concerns, particularly in respect of sexual conduct, I have adopted an even-handed approach. The results are not statistically very significant even in the context of the Gospels.

Conclusion

	S	-S	+S	P	-P	+P	J	-J	+J
Matthew	16	8	8	37	11	26	12	1	11
Mark	6	3	3	19	6	13	2	0	2
Luke	14	10	4	49	9	40	15	3	12
John	8	2	6	11	3	8	8	3	5
TOTAL	44	23	21	116	29	87	37	7	30

Although we are treating all Biblical references to be of equal weight, nonetheless there must be special attention accorded to what the Gospels say about our three issues because they are the closest documents we have to the views of Jesus.

We should note, in the first place, that on relevant citations all four Gospels score power and socio-economic justice higher than sex and gender, although John is not statistically very relevant, in a ratio of 4 : 1. As usual, the vast majority of sexual references are those which oppose adultery and there are key references where subsequent sexual relations to divorce are defined as adulterous. There are no references in the Gospels to homosexuality. Our benchmark issue of procedural justice citations out-score sex and gender.

2.2.   ACTS

Most scholars accept that the Acts of the Apostles is the second part of a two-part work (Luke/Acts) by the same author known as Luke (cf. 1.1). The attribution to Luke, a "physician" and supposed travelling companion of Paul (cf. Colossians 4.14, 2 Timothy 4.11, Philemon 24), first appears in the second century CE with Irenaeus, Tertullian, and Clement of Alexandria. It was probably composed at the turn of the first century.

At various points the narrative shifts into the first person plural but this may be to enhance verisimilitude. There are differences between accounts in Acts and other sources; one such example is as Paul (cf. Acts 15.20 and Galatians 2.10), with the latter being much more radical and 'permissive' than the former. One novel ethical, socio-economic feature is the way in which personal possessions are viewed in a 'kingdom' or near eschatological context.

2.1: +P
"They were all together in one place"; the first reference to communal living which involves the sharing and/or exchange of goods and services. This was no doubt much more common in the environment of the extended family than it is now, but it is still a remarkable socio-economic departure from the very stringent concern in the

Pentateuch for personal property, although communal ownership was observed at Qumran (1 QS 1.11). Some readers have taken this and related instances to mean that true Christian living is close in its practice to primitive, non-state communism; others believe that belief in an imminent eschaton created special conditions. The first of these arguments is not relevant to our enquiry but the second is critical, because if it is upheld, then we, and others, can claim exemption from particular or special circumstances for a great deal of what is written in Scripture, denying that it need be applied to subsequent times and other places. Thus, to take a very simple example, fundamentalist Baptists in the United States are fanatically committed to private property and would reject any notion that this verse is applicable to them, saying that it was the product of special circumstances. Yet they seek to apply to our own place and time moral strictures such as those concerning homosexuality, which might well be deeply contextual, i.e., concerned with commercial, as opposed to domestic, homosexuality. Readers will have observed that I am much more likely to see universality in socio-economic prescriptions than in those which are sexual. This is because, while the sexual frequently involves the exercise of authority and property rights in Scripture, the requirements of socio-economic justice are transparent whatever the context.

2.44–7: +P
This reference is more specific than 2.1 and goes much further than sharing, but speaks of the disposal of goods in order to assist "all, as any had need".

4.32–37: +P
cf. 2.1.

5.1–11: +P
The gruesome, caricatured story of Ananias and Sapphira which warns of the perils of apparent generosity and concealed dishonesty.

6.1–6: +P
The organisation of philanthropy and the dangerous precedent of
6.4 which separates spiritual activity, such as praying and teaching,
from physical service, although the division, in the case of Stephen
and Philip, is not upheld.

9.36–43: +P
The restoration to life by Peter of the disciple Tabitha (Dorcas),
"devoted to good works and acts of charity".

10.1: +P
Cornelius the Centurion "gave alms generously".

10.30–31: +P
Cornelius' alms have been "remembered before God".

15.20: +S
Fornication forbidden as one of the residual pillars of Judaism to
be adopted by Gentile Christians. Unless the reference to "blood"
is an injunction against murder, three pillars seem to relate to
pagan worship; the reference to fornication is therefore a somewhat
strange and awkward reference. These four pillars are a variant on
the Noachite (natural law) prohibitions to which the establishment
of procedural justice is added. This account is very different from
Paul's, cf. Galatians 2.10.

15.29: +S
cf. 15.20.

20.33–35: +P
Against covetousness and in favour of working and giving.

21.25: +S
cf. 15.20.

24.18: +P
Paul brings alms to Jerusalem; cf. Romans 15.25–29, 1 Corinthians 16.1–4, Galatians 2.10.

26.19–20: +P
"Deeds consistent with repentance". At first glance the context indicates that such deeds are connected with Temple observance, but as Gentiles appear in the list the deeds must be propitiatory in a more practical way.

Summary

	S	-S	+S	P	-P	+P	J	-J	+J
Acts	3	0	3	11	0	11	0	0	0

If, as seems most likely, the author of Acts and Luke is the same person, we would expect, on the basis of Luke, a strong bias in favour of social justice, which turns out to be the case. All three positive S references are to the minimum injunctions on Gentile Christians, including fornication. There are no references to procedural justice.

2.3.   LETTERS

Although the methodology for this enquiry is to score all citations equal in weight, it is important that, as a tool for more refined assessment, we should pay some attention to which letters were and were not written by Paul, as some will be inclined to give more weight to the former. It is also important to establish a kind of chronology for the letters to see whether there are any chronological trends.

The letters known to have been written by Paul were, in all probability, written between 40 and 65 CE and therefore some time before the first Gospel. Our ordering of letters ascribed to Paul is traditional, which places them in approximate descending order of length. Some of the later letters, known as the 'Pastoral' and 'General' letters, could have been written as late as the second quarter of the second century CE.

2.3.1.   Romans

Because of its role in Reformation theology, Paul's letter to the Romans is the most hotly contested text in Scripture. The understanding of Luther and some other Protestant reformers was that salvation could not be achieved through human conduct, no matter how good, but only through faith in God. This understandable reaction against the degradation of right living into a system of indulgences radically transferred the emphasis from Catholic corporate philanthropy to Protestant individual salvation based on Christ's atonement. Campbell has shown, to my satisfaction at least, that the best English translation is that we are saved by God's faithfulness and not our own faith.[8] An understanding of this position impinges enormously on the importance of the socio-economic aspect of the present enquiry to the extent that if one accepts the Lutheran interpretation it is so anti-Pelagian that it can be taken to rule out good works altogether.

The other issue of importance for us is the growing recognition that Romans is written in a variety of 'voices' where Paul puts counter arguments, more or less fairly, through the use of a 'devil's advocate'.[9] If this is the case, then it is much more difficult to attribute all statements in Romans to Paul. We will see that this is a critical issue in respect of key citations.

---

[8]   Douglas A. Campbell, *The Deliverance of God: An Apocalyptic Re-Reading of Justification in Paul* (Eerdmans, 2009).

[9]   cf. Campbell, op. cit., p. 542, and Levin and Brettler, op. cit., p. 257.

Romans was one of Paul's last letters, written *c.*60 CE to Gentile Christians who needed to understand how they should relate to Jewish Christians. It is often taken, as the result of severely partisan reading, to denigrate Jews, but it does quite the opposite.

1.1: +P
Paul is a servant.

1.18–28: +S
One of the key citations taken to condemn homosexuality, but which presents major problems. Firstly, Campbell demonstrates convincingly that the speaker in 1.18–31 and beyond is speech-in-character, i.e., Paul's representation (accurate or otherwise) of a false teacher.[10] Therefore, the citation cannot be taken to be Paul's view. Secondly, if the first observation is wrong and this is in fact Paul himself speaking, it is difficult to understand the process by which men and women reach the state the speaker so much decries, i.e., from pride, to idolatry, to homosexuality. Thirdly, if the process in the second point is to be taken seriously, it is difficult to see how it can be applicable either to orthodox Jews or to Christianised Jews. It must apply, then, to Gentiles, which would in itself be strange in the context of verses 1.1–17, and it does not fit well into an enquiry into the means of salvation. Alternatively, the passage might simply reflect Paul's disgust with contemporary Roman imperial sexual proclivities (cf. Habakkuk 2.4); such criticism based on Habakkuk appears in Qumran documents. Finally, whatever this passage is about, it is difficult to see how it can have any bearing upon Christians in monogamous, domestic homosexual relationships.

1.29–31: +P
A list of serious infractions, some of which are practised against the weak.

---

[10] Campbell, op. cit., p. 542, in response to the more general observation of Levine and Brettler, op. cit., p. 257.

2.1: -J
Concerning moral judgment, not procedural justice.

2.7–20: +P
A passage with strong, pragmatic overtones but I take the sense of the whole to be moralistic.

2.22: +S
Against adultery, by implication.

3.20–26: -P
The famous passage interpreted by Luther to deny the importance of "works", as opposed to "faith".

5.3–5: +P
The value of endurance and suffering; cf. Matthew 10.17–42.

6.12–19: +S
It is impossible to read this passage without identifying sexual overtones in it, even though nothing specific is said.

7.1–3: +S
An incidental reference to adultery occurring when a woman lives with another man while her husband is still alive.

7.7–8: +P
Implicit condemnation of covetousness.

8.17–23: +P
Suffering and salvation; elevating rather than pragmatic.

12.8: +P
Implicit praise of giving.

12.9–10: +S, +P, +J
Love.

12.12–13: +P
Contribute to "the saints" and be hospitable.

12.16: +P
Do not be haughty; associate with the lowly.

13.8–11: +S, +P, +J
A somewhat equivocal commentary on the concept of love, tying it, perhaps, too tightly to the Commandments, a list in which adultery is specified.

14.10–13: +J
Against moralising judgment.

15.1–6: +P
Primarily a spiritual exhortation but with just enough practical application to score.

15.25–27: +P
Paul's collection for the brethren in Jerusalem with which he was so preoccupied; I do not take this to be a mere exhortation to help religious leaders, e.g., a home for retired clergy!

16.1–3, 7: -S
Women in strong leadership roles, subsequently eliminated in the Pastoral Letters.

Summary

	S	-S	+S	P	-P	+P	J	-J	+J
Romans	7	1	6	14	1	13	4	1	3

In spite of the apparent dismissal in 3.20–26 of "works", the letter as a whole shows a substantial score for P, which makes one wonder how carefully Luther read those parts of the letter which did not immediately speak to his own personal crisis or the issue of indulgences.

2.3.2.　1 Corinthians

Paul's First Letter to the Corinthians, written in the mid-50s CE to a largely Gentile audience, impinges directly on our enquiry because much of it is taken up with gender and sexual issues. We suffer in our understanding of it more than in most cases because we can only surmise the precise terms in which issues were addressed to Paul. As Paul seems to have believed that the Eschaton was at hand, this presents a particular framework for ethical questions quite different from our own.

3.12–15: +P
Warning against wealth; partly pragmatic.

4.2: +P
Servants of Christ.

4.9–13: +P
Suffering hardship for Christ; cf. Matthew 10.17–42.

5.1–5: -S
Shock at a man living with his father's wife.

5.9–13: +S, +P
Against adultery and greed, *inter alia*.

6.1–8: -J
Against procedural justice, perhaps because it is Roman and secular, although this does not trouble Paul in Acts 25.11–12. Too often this injunction has been taken to mean that the Church should handle criminal matters, such as child abuse, within its own jurisdiction.

6.9–11: +S, +P
A list of wrong doing that will bar people from the Kingdom, including, among others: "fornicators . . . , adulterers, male prostitutes, sodomites . . . , the greedy". As there is no such thing in the Old Testament as a "Sodomite", not even applied to the inhabitants of Sodom, the history of the concept is obscure. A "male prostitute" seems to mean someone who is penetrated rather than penetrates, and a "sodomite" might be his male, sexual counterpart. However, the whole passage, as it refers to homosexuality, is unsatisfactorily messy and, like its eponymous original, Genesis 19, bears no relationship to contemporary issues.

6.13–20: +S
An unfavourable comparison of fornication with prostitutes and the relationship with God.

7.1–9: -S
Against marriage on the grounds of eschatological proximity; relatively mutual in comparison with later citations.

7.11–16: +S
Against divorce.

7.25–35: -S
A false antithesis of Christian faithfulness and marriage.

7.36–40: -S
Marriage justified to prevent fornication; merely pragmatic. It is passages like these that have not only led to the ranking of clerical celibacy above lay marriage, they have also led to a clerical aversion to sexual relationships, even within marriage. See how few marriage hymns there are in hymnals!

10.8: +S
Against sexual immorality.

10.17: +P
We are all one body because we all share in one bread.

11.3: -S
"The husband is the head of the wife . . . "

11.4–16: -S
A rather muddled passage about creation, gender, hair, and hair covering.

11.17–22: +P
Horror at social divisions during the Eucharist.

13.1–14.1: +S, +P, +J
The famous hymn to love; possesses a strong sense of the kenotic.

14.31–36: -S
Women to be silent in church; probably a later interpolation closer to sentiments in the Pastoral Epistles.

16.1–4: +P
The collection for the "saints".

16.14: +S, +P, +J
Love.

16.19: -S
A woman in a prominent role.

Summary

	S	-S	+S	P	-P	+P	J	-J	+J
1 Corinthians	15	8	7	10	0	10	3	1	2

In spite of the high score in this most obviously sex-oriented letter, P still has a higher score when comparing the plus scores.

2.3.3.   2 Corinthians

Paul writes to the Corinthians, with whom he has already been in dispute (cf. 1 Corinthians) over the collection of funds for the Jerusalem church, to re-assert his authority in the face of newly arrived opponents who question his unique status and oppose the settlement of the so-called Council of Jerusalem c.50 CE(cf. Acts 15). Although reference to previous disputes dates this material as later than 1 Corinthians, it appears to be a collection of whole or parts of letters. A mass of material is inserted between 2.12 and 7.5; 6.14–7-1 does not read like Paul, displaying an uncharacteristic dualism and appearing to have been inserted arbitrarily, interrupting the flow; 8–9 appear to be totally separate letters. The customary division of chapters and verses is not simply misleading, it is a complete mess!

1.6–11: +P
The centrality of suffering in discipleship. Scores plus because suffering involves both material deprivation and a loss of power; cf. Matthew 10.17–42.

2.4: +S, +P, +J
Love.

2.8: +S, +P, +J
Love.

4.7–12: +P
cf. 1.6–11.

4.16–17: +P
cf. 1.6–11.

5.1–5: +P
cf. 1.6–11.

5.6–10: -P
Refers to the spiritual, not bodily deprivation.

5.14: +S, +P, +J
Love.

6.4–10: +P
cf. 1.6–11.

7.5: +P
cf. 1.6–11.

8: +S, +P, +J
Emphasises not only generosity but also self-sacrifice in giving, but then emphasises a balance between generosity and prudence. Overall, scores positive. Additional S and J scores because of the use of "love" in 8.7.

9: +P
A second plea for the collection for the "saints".

11.2: -S
The comparison of the man to the woman as Christ to his Church, stated here in simple form, is perhaps the most disastrously misogynistic metaphor in the whole of the New Testament. As the Church is in a different category from Christ, i.e., intractably inferior, to say this of a woman in relation to her husband is to place her almost beyond relationship and certainly in a position of complete obedience. Given 1 Corinthians 7, and even more so 16.1, it is highly likely that in the attempt to pay a rather clumsy compliment; presumably Paul did not realise his blunder.

11.23–29: +P
Paul recounts his sufferings in following Christ as a proof of superiority over his impostor rivals.

12.6–10: +P
In praise of weakness.

12.15: +S, +P, +J
Love.

12.20–21: +S, +P
A list of infractions including jealousy and sexual wrong-doing.

Summary

	S	-S	+S	P	-P	+P	J	-J	+J
2 Corinthians	7	1	6	16	1	15	5	0	5

A huge differential between relevant S and P scores, overshadowed, however, by 11.2.

2.3.4.   Galatians

We have already seen opposition to Paul being a factor in Romans and 2 Corinthians, but nowhere is this more obvious than in his Letter to the Galatians, where the apparent aggression of his conservative opponents leads him into a much less nuanced view of Judaism than that which he so carefully prepared in Romans. Scholarly opinion on the dating of the letter varies between the mid-40s and mid-50s CE, but in any case this crude expression of the position of Judaism, and the relationship between faith and works, noted in the introduction to Romans (Section 2.3.1, p. 116), precedes the more nuanced approach.

2.1–10: +P
Cf Acts 15. Paul's account of the so-called Council of Jerusalem is radically simpler than the account in Acts, and whereas the latter's emphasis is on the similarities and differences between traditional Judaism and emerging Christianity, Paul's account is radically socio-economic.

3.28: -S
A strong affirmation of gender equality; somewhat at odds with 2 Corinthians 11.2, subsequently undermined in the Pastoral Letters.

5.13–15: +S, +P, +J
Love.

5.19–21: +S, +P
A list of vices including sexual and economic.

5.22–23: +S, +P, +J
List of virtues including love.

6.10: +P
"Let us work for the good of all, and especially for those of the family of faith".

6.16: +J
Mercy.

Summary

	S	-S	+S	P	-P	+P	J	-J	+J
Galatians	4	1	3	5	0	5	3	0	3

Low scores for all categories in a letter concerned with other issues.

2.3.5.   Ephesians

Traditionally, Ephesians, together with Philippians, Colossians, and Philemon, were known as the 'Captivity Epistles' because they were supposed to have been written by Paul from his prison in Rome. However, most scholars now agree that this letter (if it is indeed a letter rather than a sermon and if it is addressed to the Ephesians, which is doubtful) is pseudepigraphic, like Colossians to which it bears a close resemblance.. Like later non-Pauline Epistles, Ephesians is keen to emphasise the subservient role of women.

1.15: +S, +P, +J
Love.

3.13: +P
The writer's suffering.

3.17: +S, +P, +J
Love.

4.1: +P
Imprisoned.

4.2: +S, +P, +J
Love

4.15–16: +S, +P, +J
Love.

4.19: +S, +P
A description of Gentile immorality.

5.2: +S, +P, +J
Love.

5.3–5: +S, +P
Against fornication and greed.

5.21–32: -S
This is a more misogynistic formulation than that in 1 Corinthians 7, but less so than 2 Corinthians 11.2. The injunction that husbands must love their wives—as everybody must love everybody—hardly compensates for the intrinsic female inferiority. There is a sense near the end of the passage that the author is trying to mitigate earlier forcefulness.

Summary

	S	-S	+S	P	-P	+P	J	-J	+J
Ephesians	8	1	7	9	0	9	5	0	5

Plus scores more or less even but, again, overshadowed, this time by 5.21–32.

2.3.6. Philippians

Philippians was probably written by Paul from Ephesus in the mid-50s CE rather than from a Roman prison in the early 60s; the journeys Paul mentions (cf. 2.19, 23–30, 4.18) and the presence of Timothy (cf. 1.1) are suggestive. Some scholars identify two, or even three, separate letters. Paul's opponents are still in evidence, cf. 1.15–17.

1.9: +S, +P, +J
Love.

1.29: +P
Suffering for Christ; cf. Matthew 10.17–42.

2.1–2: +S, +P, +J
Love.

2.3–5: +P
Exhortations to humility and selflessness and against selfish ambition.

2.6–11: -S, -P, -J
Possibly the most important and most overlooked passage in the whole of the New Testament. It inverts love from the positive virtues of self-control (S), caring (P), and fairness (J) to *kenosis*, the paradox of active passivism and self-giving by being receptive to the other. It may appear slightly perverse to score this negative but I see no other logical alternative.

2.17: +P
Suffering for Christ; cf. Matthew 10.17–42.

3.8.: +P
cf. 2.17.

4.6: +P
"Do not worry about anything" surely has an element of earthly concerns.

4.11–13: +P
"I have learned to be content with whatever I have".

4.14–18: +P
Thanks to Philippians for sharing Paul's distress.

Summary

	S	-S	+S	P	-P	+P	J	-J	+J
Philippians	3	0	3	11	0	11	0	0	0

A substantial differential in favour of P over S.

2.3.7.   Colossians

Most scholars agree that Colossians was written a generation after Paul, using his well-known theological language but departing from his theology of salvation (cf. 3.1–14). Even more striking is the earliest reference in the New Testament to the hierarchical household; compare Colossians 3.22–24 with 1 Corinthians 7.1–4. Paul's stance, formulated in the eschatological shadow, gave way to a less egalitarian outlook as that shadow faded; cf. Ephesians 6.5–9, Titus 2.3–5, 1 Timothy 6.1–2, and 1 Peter 2.18–21. There is much shared content with Ephesians, another pseudepigraphic letter. The author flatly contradicts Paul's position on the relationship of Gentiles to Judaism which further indicates composition long after Paul's death.

1.8: +S, +P, +J
Love

1.11: +P
In praise of endurance.

1.24–25: +P
Rejoicing in suffering and service; cf. Matthew 10.17–42.

2.2: +S, +P, +J
Love.

3.2: +P
"Set your mind on things that are above, not on things that are on earth".

3.5–10: +S, +P
A list of vices including fornication and greed.

3.13: +P, +J
A list of virtues including kindness and humility.

3.14: +S, +P, +J
Love.

3.18–19: -S
Wives to obey husbands, husbands to love wives and not treat them harshly; cf. 1 Corinthians 8, 11.3; 2 Corinthians 11.2.

4.15: -S
A woman of influence.

Summary

	S	-S	+S	P	-P	+P	J	-J	+J
Colossians	6	2	4	8	0	8	4	0	4

2.3.8.   1 Thessalonians

Paul's First Letter to the Thessalonians, written *c*.50 CE, is his first extant letter and, therefore, the earliest document of the New Testament. Acts 17.1–10 and 1 Thessalonians disagree on some points, which brings the former into doubt more than the latter. After reviewing the history of the new Church, the over-riding concern is the *Parousia*, or the coming of the final judgment.

1.3: +S, +P, +J
It is encouraging to note how early the concept of love occurs in this earliest document of the New Testament.

2.2: +P
Suffered and mistreated for Christ; cf. Matthew 10.17–42.

2.14: +P
The Thessalonians suffered for their faith.

3.12: +S, +P, +J
Love.

4.3–8: +S
Fornication is associated with Gentiles.

4.9–10: +S, +P, +J
Love.

5.8: +S, +P, +J
Love.

5.13: +S, +P, +J
Love

5.14: +P
Help the weak may refer to faith, but I take it in context to be broader.

Summary

	S	-S	+S	P	-P	+P	J	-J	+J
1 Thessalonians	6	0	6	8	0	8	5	0	5

2.3.9.   2 Thessalonians

Scholars are divided on the authorship of this letter but its extended eschatological time-frame, as opposed to the imminence and uncertainty in 1 Thessalonians, seems to arise from a later date. It would not be difficult to identify the problems dealt with in the letter, using Paul's authority, with an outbreak of eschatological enthusiasm in the context of a settling Church. If the letter is authentic it was probably written in the early 50s CE.

1.3: +S, +P, +J
Love.

1.4–6: +P
Afflictions suffered for the faith.

Summary

	S	-S	+S	P	-P	+P	J	-J	+J
2 Thessalonians	1	0	1	2	0	2	1	0	1

2.3.10. 1 Timothy

1/2 Timothy and Titus are known as the Pastoral Epistles because they are largely concerned with the conduct of Christian communities. The language of justification, faith, and eschatology is replaced by an emphasis on moral rectitude, orthodoxy, and— this is the clue to the date of authorship—tradition. The likeliest date of authorship is the turn of the first century CE. It is unlikely that Paul, writing almost half a century earlier, would have so radically altered his view from, say, 1 Corinthians, and it is unlikely that by the early 60s the growing Church had reached the point of ecclesiastical development described in 1 Timothy.

1.2: +J
Mercy.

1.5: +S, +P, +J
Love

1.8–11: +S, +J
The importance of the law, not least against fornicators and sodomites. It is likely that these were Gentiles.

2.8–15: +S, +P, -S
A complex passage with a predominantly misogynistic tone. This flatly contradicts Galatians 3.28 and Romans 16.1–3, 7 which show women in leadership roles, but is consistent with 1 Corinthians 14.31–36 which many scholars consider to be a post Pauline interpolation. Female subordination is grounded in Creation where Eve is given all the responsibility for the departure from Eden (cf. Genesis 3).

3.2: -S
A bishop must only be married once, in contradiction to traditional polygamy; cf. Genesis 28.9.

3.3–6: +P
A bishop, among other things, must neither be a lover of money nor conceited.

3.8: +P
Deacons, among other things, must not be greedy.

3.11: -S
The wives of deacons must be well behaved.

3.12: -S
Deacons must only be married once; cf. 3.2.

4.3: -S
Opposition to marriage is false teaching; perhaps the emergence of Gnosticism.

4.7: -S
"Old wives tales . . . "; a revealing piece of gratuitous misogyny!

4.10: +P
Toil and struggle.

4.12: +S, +P, +J
Love.

5.2: -S
Proper address to older and younger women.

5.3–16: -S
A quite remarkable and apparently disproportionate attack on widowhood; contains much misogynistic caricature.

6.2–10: +P
A passage against the evils of money, tinged with pragmatism but essentially moralistic.

6.11: +S, +P, +J
Love.

6.17–19: +P
cf. 6.2–10.

Summary

	S	-S	+S	P	-P	+P	J	-J	+J
1 Timothy	13	8	5	9	0	9	5	0	5

Even in this most self-consciously sex- and gender-focused letter, ushering in a more misogynistic tone, the total S references outweigh the total P references. Nonetheless, the relevant P references are more than twice the S references.

2.3.11. 2 Timothy

All that was written in the Introduction to 1 Timothy also applies to 2 Timothy. Apocryphal Christian writings at the turn of the century often support female celibacy and are strongly misogynistic, which only serves to confirm earlier remarks.

1.1: +J
Mercy.

1.16–18: +J
Mercy.

2.9–12: +P
Suffering and endurance for the Gospel; cf. Matthew 10.17–42.

2.22: +S, +P, +J
Love.

3.2: +P
Lovers of money condemned.

3.6–9: -S
"Silly women . . . swayed by all kinds of desires". Need I say more?!

3.10: +S, +P, +J
Love.

4.6–9: +P
Timothy is to endure suffering just as the author has endured suffering.

4.19: -S
The requirement of authenticity over-rides misogyny!

Summary

	S	-S	+S	P	-P	+P	J	-J	+J
2 Timothy	4	2	2	5	0	5	4	0	4

2.3.12. Titus

Most scholars accept that this Letter to Titus is pseudepigraphic (see the introduction to 1 Timothy, Section 2.3.10, p. 133). The letter displays striking Hellenistic influences and it strongly relates social behaviour to ethics.

1.6: -S
A bishop must be married only once; cf. 1 Timothy 3.2.

1.7: +P
cf. 1 Timothy 3.3–6.

1.11: -P
I take this to be exaggerated and not ethical teaching on wealth.

2.2: +S, +P, +J
Love.

2.3–5: -S
Another passage implying moral weakness based on gender.

3.8: +P
In praise of good works.

3.15: +S, +P, +J
Love.

Summary

	S	-S	+S	P	-P	+P	J	-J	+J
Titus	4	2	2	5	1	4	2	0	2

2.3.13. Philemon

This letter of Paul, written from prison, possibly at Ephesus, is one of the three Captivity Letters, (see the introduction to Ephesians, Section 2.3.5, p. 127), dating from the mid-50s CE.

1: -S
"Apphia our sister".

5: +S, +P, +J
Love.

7: +S, +P, +J
Love.

9: +S, +P, +J
Love.

Summary

	S	-S	+S	P	-P	+P	J	-J	+J
Philemon	4	1	3	3	0	3	3	0	3

2.3.14. Hebrews

In many ways the most mysterious document in the New Testament, it is not known when Hebrews was written (before or after the destruction of the Temple in 70 CE), by whom, from where, to whom, and in what genre (letter or homily). It is the most sophisticated composition in the New Testament, with discernible Platonic influences. It is the first recorded coherent argument concerning the nature of Christ, advocating a 'high' Christology. Ethics are merely incidental.

2.18: +P
Being tested for Christ; cf. Matthew 10.17–42, Exodus 15.25, Deuteronomy 8.2, Proverbs 3.11–12.

6.10: +S, +P, +J
Love in serving "the saints".

8.12: +J
God's mercy.

10.18: +J
Forgiveness rather than sacrifices; cf. Matthew 9.13

10.24: +S, +P, +J
Love

10.24: +P
Good deeds.

10.26–31: -J
Apparently in contradiction to 10.18, as if Christ's redemption only works once.

10.32–39: +P
An affirmation of suffering and generosity.

11.31: -S
Another glowing tribute to Rahab the Prostitute; cf. Joshua 2.1–21, 6.17, 22–23, 25.

11.32–40: -P
A powerful passage recounting suffering for God, but scored negative because it refers to Old Testament suffering, not suffering for Christ.

12: -P, -J
This does not appear to be suffering for others but, rather, suffering from sin. A repetition of retributive justice; cf. 10.26–31.

13.1–4: +P
Compassion for prisoners, etc.

13.5: +S
Against fornication and adultery but dropped into the text out of context.

13.6: +P
Against money and greed.

13.16: +P
Sacrifice, share, and do good.

Summary

	S	-S	+S	P	-P	+P	J	-J	+J
Hebrews	4	1	3	10	2	8	6	2	4

2.3.15. James

James is the first of the 'General Epistles', which is to say, those addressed to the early Church but to no community in particular. The Greek makes it difficult to imagine that it was written by James, the Brother of Jesus(see Matthew 13.55; Mark 6.3) and the head of the Jerusalem Church (see Acts 12.17, 15.13–21; Galatians 1.19) although some scholars maintain that it could have been dictated to a learned scribe. The main argument of the letter or homily is in support of good works and ethical behaviour, apparently in the light of Romans. Consequently, Luther and some other reformers wished to exclude it from the canonical Scriptures.

1.2–5: +P
In praise of endurance for Christ; cf. Matthew 10.17–42, also Psalm 11.5.

1.9–11: +P
Praise for the lowly and warning to the rich.

1.21: +P
In praise of meekness.

1.22–25: +P
"Be doers of the Word, not merely hearers".

1.27: +P
Widows and orphans.

2.1–9: +P
The example of fair treatment for the poor man *vis à vis* the rich man; cf. Deuteronomy 16.19, Matthew 5.3, Luke 6.20.

2.11–12: +S
The seriousness of adultery.

2.13: +J
"Mercy triumphs over judgment"; cf. Micah 7.19–20.

2.14–26: -S, +P
Faith without works is useless. This is the passage that most offended Martin Luther who put it in opposition to Romans 3.20–28. Another nice reference to Rahab the prostitute!

3.13–17: +P, +J
In praise of good works and earthly virtues, including justice.

4.3: -P
Not specific enough to score.

4.4: -S
Use of "adulterer" to mean wrong-doer.

4.6: +P
Against pride and in favour of humility; cf. Proverbs 3.34.

4.10: +P
cf. 4.6.

4.12: +J
Against judgment.

5.1–5: +P
The rich are called upon to weep and wail; cf. Matthew 19.23, Luke 6.24–25.

5.11: +P
In favour of endurance.

Summary

	S	-S	+S	P	-P	+P	J	-J	+J
James	3	2	1	13	1	12	3	0	3

As we would expect from its introduction, there is a very high P score.

2.3.16. 1 Peter

1 Peter was almost certainly not written by Peter but little else can be said about it.

1.6–7: +P
 In praise of endurance.

1.22: +S, +P, +J
Love.

2.17: +S, +P, +J
Love.

2.18–23: +P
In praise of endurance, likened to Christ.

3.1–7: -S
Wives to obey husbands, dress modestly, etc.; husbands simply to "show consideration for . . . the weaker sex"; cf. 1 Corinthians 11.3, 2 Corinthians 11.2, 1 Timothy, 2.9–15. There is, perhaps, a stronger emphasis on the submissive wife as the result of contact with Greco-Roman practice.

3.8: +S, +P, +J
Love, and humility.

3.17: +P
The virtue of suffering.

4.1: +P
Suffering; cf. 3.17.
   +S
   +P

4.8: +J
Love.

4.13: +P
Rejoice in sharing Christ's sufferings.

4.19: +P
cf. 3.17.

5.2: +P
Against sordid gain.

5.5–6: +P
In praise of humility; cf. Proverbs 3.34.

Summary

	S	-S	+S	P	-P	+P	J	-J	+J
1 Peter	5	1	4	12	0	12	4	0	4

The high score for P is not only accounted for by the use of the term "love", which accounts for all the J references, but also because of the underlying issue of persecution which required endurance and suffering.

2.3.17. 2 Peter

Again, like 1 Peter, this letter was probably not written by Peter but might have been written as late as the middle of the second century CE. It is strongly dependent on the Letter of Jude, is concerned with orthodoxy, and refers to a collection of Paul's writings; the opponents which it warns against appear to be Gnostics.

1.6–8: +S, +P, +J
Endurance and love.

2.6–13: -S
Sodom and Gomorrah are "ungodly"; cf. Genesis 13.13, 19.4–11. However, there is a later specification that the false prophets have "indulged their flesh in depraved lust" (2.10), which might refer to Genesis 19.4–11, but more likely refers to Judges 19; 2 Peter appears to be concerned with the violation of hospitality as found in the latter, rather than the homosexuality implied in the former. Indeed, this passage is extremely inflammatory; you can imagine a "false prophet" preaching wrong doctrine, but any individual as wicked as described would not be mistaken for a prophet at all! Strong evidence here of the late date of the letter.

2.14: +S, +P
Against the "eyes full of adultery" and the greed of these "false prophets".

2.18: +S
Against "licentious desires of the flesh".

Summary

	S	-S	+S	P	-P	+P	J	-J	+J
2 Peter	4	1	3	2	0	2	1	0	1

2.3.18. 1 John

Although there is much in the language and style of the three Letters of John which bears a relationship to the Gospel of John, most scholars now account for this by positing the theory that there was a 'Johannine school', perhaps in Ephesus, at the beginning of the second century CE. The acrimonious schism (cf. 2.19) appears to concern Docetism.

2.10: +S, +P, +J
Love.

2.16: +S, +P
The reference against "the flesh" might be general but in this context it looks sexual; "pride in riches" is much clearer.

3.11–24: +S, +P, +J
Love.

4.7–21: +S, +P, +J
Love.

5.1–4: +S, +P, +J
In this passage on love, there is the limiting factor that it is tied to the commandments, which would rule out P and J. I have taken the view that it is best to score "love" in all three categories, even if this proportionately, though not absolutely, favours S and J.

Summary

	S	-S	+S	P	-P	+P	J	-J	+J
1 John	5	0	5	5	0	5	4	0	4

The close scoring is accounted for by the predominance of "love".

2.3.19. 2 John

As in the introduction to 1 John, reference to "the elder" makes it even less likely that this Letter was written by an original follower of Jesus.

1–6: +S, +P, +J
Love.

Summary

	S	-S	+S	P	-P	+P	J	-J	+J
2 John	1	0	1	1	0	1	1	0	1

2.3.20. 3 John

See the introductions to 1/2 John.

6: +S, +P, +J
Love.

Summary

	S	-S	+S	P	-P	+P	J	-J	+J
3 John	1	0	1	1	0	1	1	0	1

2.3.21. Jude

This final General Epistle's claim to have been written by Judas, brother of Jesus, is not very strong, although some scholars propose its authorship in the 50s CE.

2: +S, +P, +J
Love.

4–12: +S
A brutal attack on "false prophets", i.e., unorthodox teachers, against whom the ultimate condemnation appears to be against homosexuality, although it might be of a specialist kind, i.e., desiring sexual intercourse with angels (cf. Genesis 19.4–11). Alternatively, the passage might refer to unhealthy spiritual practices. Indeed, the whole chain of homosexual references, starting at Genesis 19.4–11, may well refer to the angelic special case or be a metaphor for unsound practice. It is difficult to imagine that the author has a stable, domestic relationship in mind. Only marginally a plus score.

Summary

	S	-S	+S	P	-P	+P	J	-J	+J
Jude	2	0	2	1	0	1	1	0	1

Conclusion

	S	-S	+S	P	-P	+P	J	-J	+J
Romans	7	1	6	14	1	13	4	1	3
1 Corinthians	15	8	7	10	0	10	3	1	2
2 Corinthians	7	1	6	16	1	15	5	0	5
Galatians	4	1	3	5	0	5	3	0	3
Ephesians	8	1	7	9	0	9	5	0	5
Philippians	3	1	2	10	1	9	3	1	2
Colossians	6	2	4	8	0	8	4	0	4
1 Thessalonians	6	0	6	8	0	8	5	0	5
2 Thessalonians	1	0	1	2	0	2	1	0	1
1 Timothy	13	8	5	9	0	9	5	0	5

	S	-S	+S	P	-P	+P	J	-J	+J
2 Timothy	4	2	2	5	0	5	4	0	4
Titus	4	2	2	5	1	4	2	0	2
Philemon	4	1	3	3	0	3	3	0	3
Hebrews	4	1	3	10	2	8	6	2	4
James	3	2	1	13	1	12	3	0	3
1 Peter	5	1	4	12	0	12	4	0	4
2 Peter	4	1	3	2	0	2	1	0	1
1 John	5	0	5	5	0	5	4	0	4
2 John	1	0	1	1	0	1	1	0	1
3 John	1	0	1	1	0	1	1	0	1
Jude	2	0	2	1	0	1	1	0	1
TOTAL	107	33	74	149	7	142	68	5	63

In spite of an increasingly misogynistic tone as we proceed through the letters, the overall score for power and wealth still outstrips that for sex and gender by 3 : 2, with justice and mercy substantially below that. However, when we look at relevant references, the ratio in favour of P over S is 2 : 1, with J not too far behind.

Although we have noted this before, it is important to emphasise that the largest number of relevant S scores are against fornication or adultery. The next largest S group is simply associated with "love". If we were to eliminate all the S, P and J scores associated with "love", the absolute scores would be uniformly reduced but the ratio in favour of P would increase.

2.4.   THE BOOK OF REVELATION

There is no evidence that the Revelation to John relates to any other New Testament work, although it shares features with near contemporary works such as Baruch and Ezra. Some date this work to the reign of Nero, others to Domitian, and yet others hold that it is a work of many hands and some generations. Its unity of style as apocalypse and prophesy, vision and letter, song and list, oracle and narrative, and the lack of any textual evidence to the contrary, indicate the intricate work of a single author. It is a matter of deep regret that this concluding work of the New Testament should contain passages of horrific misogyny (cf. Ezekiel 23).

2.2–3: +P
The endurance of the Church of Ephesus.

2.4: +S, +P, +J
To condemn the abandonment of love is to praise love.

2.8: +P
The Church of Smyrna praised for its affliction and poverty.

2.10: +P
The threat of suffering and imprisonment lauded.

2.14: -S
I take "fornication" here to be idolatry.

2.19: +S, +P, +J
Love.

2.19: +P
Thyatira's endurance.

2.21–22: -S
cf. 2.14, fornication and adultery as idolatry; one of the episodes of brutal misogyny.

3.10: +P
The patient endurance of Sardis.

3.16–18: +P
The Laodiceans rebuked for putting earthly above divine riches.

6.9: +P
Martyrdom, the ultimate sacrifice and renunciation of power, although the citation is somewhat tarnished by the call for revenge!

9.21: +S
Based on previous citations, it would appear that fornication refers to idolatry but here the context is not clear, so scored positive; cf. Ezekiel 8–9, Isaiah 54.9–20.

11.8: -S
Sodom seems to have lost any particularity of meaning; nonetheless, cf. Ezekiel 16.46–56, Isaiah 1.10, Jeremiah 23.14.

12.1–5: -S

12.13–18: -S
Two passages frequently taken to refer to Mary, the mother of Jesus, although the reference to the child "who is to rule all the nations with a rod of iron" is somewhat anomalous.

13.10: +P
The endurance of the saints.

14.1–5: +S
cf. 7.1–10, 1 Samuel 21.1–5. A notion of purity has been broadened to connect salvation with celibacy, offering a vision of angelic (not human) purity, echoing Qumran. Perhaps the origin of the move towards male clerical celibacy, but certainly a very negative comment on marriage; scored positive because citations like this explain the Church's muddle over sexuality.

14.8: -S
cf. 2.14. Based on Isaiah 21.9.

14.12–13: +S, +P
A call for the endurance of the saints; an additional S as the Commandments are specified, including adultery.

17.1–18.10: -S
cf. Ezekiel 23. A curious metaphor, where Babylon is taken to be Rome, because the supposed seduction by women has to be set against male rulers in Babylon and Rome. Initially concerned with religious purity, the lengthy passage is an ominous conflation of evil, seduction and womanhood.

18.11–23: +P
Against wealth.

19.2: -S
cf. 2.14.

19.7–10: -S
cf. 2 Corinthians 11.2. The marriage of the lamb to those who are virtuous, i.e., his bride, the Church; a reinforcement of the inferiority of women.

21.2: -S
cf. 19.7–10 Jerusalem (the Church), a bride.

21.8: +S
Literally fornicators.

21.9–27: -S
cf. 19.7–10.

22.15: +S
cf. 21.8.

22.17: -S
cf. 19.7–10.

Summary

	S	-S	+S	P	-P	+P	J	-J	+J
Revelation	19	12	7	12	0	12	2	0	2

Even in this book which is obsessed with female sexuality, bodily fluids, and pollution, the theme of endurance still holds a dominant place.

2.5. THE NEW TESTAMENT RECKONING

	S	-S	+S	P	-P	+P	J	-J	+J
Gospels	44	23	21	116	29	87	37	7	30
Acts	3	0	3	11	0	11	0	0	0
Letters	107	33	74	149	7	142	68	5	63
Revelation	19	12	7	12	0	12	2	0	2
TOTAL	173	68	105	288	36	252	107	12	95

In all the genre lines above, the total number of S references is less than the total number of P references; the ratio in favour of P over S is highest in Acts(on a small sample) but almost 3 : 1 in the Gospels. The total J references show our benchmark lagging far behind. When we look at relevant scores, the ratio rises in favour of P over S to 5 : 2 and J has almost caught up with S.

For the authors of the New Testament it is clear that issues of power and wealth far outweigh those of sex and gender, and that when we look at references relevant to our enquiry, J is not very far behind S. In terms of future discussion, it is again relevant to note the overwhelming condemnation of fornication and adultery. With reference to the S sub-set concerned with homosexuality, the

Gospels and Acts are silent but there are references, more or less ambiguous, in the Letters and Revelation.

3. SUMMARY TABLES

3.1. THE OLD TESTAMENT

3.1.1. The Pentateuch

	S	-S	+S	P	-P	+P	J	-J	+J
Genesis	23	17	6	0	0	0	0	0	0
Exodus	3	2	1	7	0	7	3	0	3
Leviticus	11	7	4	7	0	7	3	0	3
Numbers	7	7	0	0	0	0	0	0	0
Deuteronomy	17	13	4	11	3	8	3	1	2
TOTAL	61	46	15	25	3	22	9	1	8

3.1.2. The Narratives

	S	-S	+S	P	-P	+P	J	-J	+J
Joshua	5	5	0	0	0	0	0	0	0
Judges	12	12	0	0	0	0	0	0	0
Ruth	1	1	0	1	0	1	0	0	0
1 Samuel	4	3	1	1	0	1	0	0	0
2 Samuel	6	5	1	1	0	1	0	0	0
1 Kings	8	8	0	0	0	0	0	0	0
2 Kings	2	2	0	0	0	0	0	0	0

	S	-S	+S	P	-P	+P	J	-J	+J
1 Chronicles	2	2	0	0	0	0	0	0	0
2 Chronicles	2	2	0	0	0	0	0	0	0
Esther	3	3	0	0	0	0	0	0	0
Ezra	1	1	0	0	0	0	0	0	0
Nehemiah	1	1	0	1	0	1	1	0	1
TOTAL	47	45	2	4	0	4	1	0	1

3.1.3.   Wisdom Literature

	S	-S	+S	P	-P	+P	J	-J	+J
Job	3	1	2	6	0	6	0	0	0
Psalms	1	0	1	14	0	14	7	1	6
Proverbs	17	12	5	22	6	16	8	1	7
Ecclesiastes	3	2	1	1	1	0	0	0	0
Song of Songs	0	0	0	0	0	0	0	0	0
TOTAL	24	15	9	43	7	36	15	2	13

3.1.4.   The Prophets

	S	-S	+S	P	-P	+P	J	-J	+J
Isiah	7	7	0	15	0	15	20	2	18
Jeremiah	3	2	1	8	1	7	5	0	5
Lamentations	0	0	0	0	0	0	0	0	0
Ezekiel	10	6	4	6	0	6	4	0	4
Daniel	2	2	0	0	0	0	1	0	1
Hosea	4	3	1	2	0	2	1	0	1
Joel	1	0	1	0	0	0	0	0	0

	S	-S	+S	P	-P	+P	J	-J	+J
Amos	1	1	0	5	0	5	2	0	2
Obadiah	0	0	0	0	0	0	0	0	0
Jonah	0	0	0	0	0	0	0	0	0
Micah	1	1	0	1	0	1	1	0	1
Nahum	0	0	0	0	0	0	0	0	0
Habakkuk	0	0	0	0	0	0	0	0	0
Zephaniah	0	0	0	0	0	0	0	0	0
Haggai	0	0	0	0	0	0	0	0	0
Zechariah	2	2	0	1	0	1	2	0	2
Malachi	1	1	0	1	0	1	0	0	0
TOTAL	32	25	7	39	1	38	36	3	33

Summary

	S	-S	+S	P	-P	+P	J	-J	+J
Pentatuch	61	46	15	25	3	22	9	1	8
Narratives	47	45	2	4	0	4	1	0	1
Wisdom	54	15	9	43	7	36	15	2	13
Prophets	32	25	7	39	1	38	36	3	33
TOTAL	164	131	33	111	11	100	61	6	55

3.2. THE APOCRYPHA

	S	-S	+S	P	-P	+P	J	-J	+J
Tobit	1	0	1	7	0	7	1	0	1
Wisdom of Solomon	4	4	0	4	1	3	2	0	2
Sirach	21	14	7	19	3	16	4	0	4

	S	-S	+S	P	-P	+P	J	-J	+J
Baruch	0	0	0	1	0	1	0	0	0
1 Esdras	3	3	0	0	0	0	0	0	0
2 Esdras	2	2	0	2	1	1	0	0	0
Letter of Jeremiah	1	1	0	0	0	0	0	0	0
Song of Three Jews	0	0	0	0	0	0	0	0	0
Susanna	1	0	1	0	0	0	0	0	0
Bel and the Dragon	0	0	0	0	0	0	0	0	0
1 Maccabees	0	0	0	1	0	1	0	0	0
2 Maccabees	1	1	0	0	0	0	0	0	0
3 Maccabees	0	0	0	0	0	0	0	0	0
4 Maccabees	5	4	1	1	0	1	1	0	1
Manasseh	0	0	0	0	0	0	0	0	0
TOTAL	39	29	10	35	5	30	8	0	8

3.3.   THE NEW TESTAMENT

3.3.1.   The Gospels

	S	-S	+S	P	-P	+P	J	-J	+J
Matthew	16	8	8	37	11	26	12	1	11
Mark	6	3	3	19	6	13	2	0	2
Luke	14	10	4	49	9	40	15	3	12
John	8	2	6	11	3	8	8	3	5
TOTAL	44	23	21	116	29	87	37	7	30

3.3.2. Acts

	S	-S	+S	P	-P	+P	J	-J	+J
Acts	3	0	3	11	0	11	0	0	0

3.3.3. The Letters

	S	-S	+S	P	-P	+P	J	-J	+J
Romans	7	1	6	14	1	13	4	1	3
1 Corinthians	15	8	7	10	0	10	3	1	2
2 Corinthians	7	1	6	16	1	15	5	0	5
Galatians	4	1	3	5	0	5	3	0	3
Ephesians	8	1	7	9	0	9	5	0	5
Philippians	3	1	2	10	1	9	3	1	2
Colossians	6	2	4	8	0	8	4	0	4
1 Thessalonians	6	0	6	8	0	8	5	0	5
2 Thessalonians	1	0	1	2	0	2	1	0	1
1 Timothy	13	8	5	9	0	9	5	0	5
2 Timothy	4	2	2	5	0	5	4	0	4
Titus	4	2	2	5	1	4	2	0	2
Philemon	4	1	3	3	0	3	3	0	3
Hebrews	4	1	3	10	2	8	6	2	4
James	3	2	1	13	1	12	3	0	3
1 Peter	5	1	4	12	0	12	4	0	4
2 Peter	4	1	3	2	0	2	1	0	1
1 John	5	0	5	5	0	5	4	0	4
2 John	1	0	1	1	0	1	1	0	1
3 John	1	0	1	1	0	1	1	0	1
Jude	2	0	2	1	0	1	1	0	1
TOTAL	107	33	74	149	7	142	68	5	63

3.3.4. Revelation

	S	-S	+S	P	-P	+P	J	-J	+J
Revelation	19	12	7	12	0	12	2	0	2

Summary

	S	-S	+S	P	-P	+P	J	-J	+J
Gospels	44	23	21	116	29	87	37	7	30
Acts	3	0	3	11	0	11	0	0	0
Letters	107	33	74	149	7	142	68	5	63
Revelation	19	12	7	12	0	12	2	0	2
TOTAL	173	68	105	288	36	252	107	12	95

3.4.   FINAL SUMMARY

	S	-S	+S	P	-P	+P	J	-J	+J
Old Testament	164	131	33	111	11	100	61	6	55
New Testament	173	68	105	288	36	252	107	12	95
TOTAL	337	199	138	399	47	352	168	18	150

3.5.   CONCLUSION

First of all, to put our enquiry into perspective, there are only some 900 citations in the whole of the Bible on the three major topics under scrutiny out of 31,273 verses in the Bible (depending on your version). As some of our citations are lengthy, it is not possible, without much additional labour, to arrive at a precise percentage, but I think this unnecessary. The major numbers speak for themselves. Even if we had collected all the citations for love of neighbour *vis à vis* love of God, we would have found that the latter is overwhelmingly predominant. The idea, then, that the Bible is primarily an ethical manual is incorrect.

Secondly, when we examine the ethical data, even in respect of our somewhat narrow enquiry, it is clear that much of what the Bible has to say is not directly relevant to our contemporary concerns. This is why we have so many references rated minus, i.e., not relevant. In the area of sex and gender, some three fourths of citations in the Pentateuch are not relevant, referring, for example, to polygamy and Levirate marriage, and there are only two relevant references in the Narratives. Indeed, if one was to take one area of ethical and cultural life and seek guidance from the Bible, sex and gender would be the most inappropriate. As always, we have, as a Christian tradition, changed our attitude over time to what we think the Bible tells us—we are as opposed to polygamy as we are to slavery—and nowhere is this more clear than in our changing attitude to fornication and adultery. As we will see, the former is now treated by many Christians with sympathy while the latter—in the guise of divorce and re-marriage—is sanctioned, albeit with face-saving caveats. There are no citations which specifically refer either to abortion or to contraception, although there is a general presumption against them both, as one would expect of a product of an era suffering high infant mortality,. It should be noted that Jews and Christians resisted the temptation to conform to the infanticidal traditions of many of their neighbours and conquerors.

Thirdly, it is very difficult to establish a clear distinction between a theology of gender and a culture of misogyny. This is not to say that there are not those who have established a theology of gender to their satisfaction, but it is difficult to avoid the tendency, throughout the Bible, to regard women as in some ways inferior to men, which must present any gender theology with the task of heavy discounting. As I have pointed out in the notes on citations, Genesis 3.16 operates in rather peculiar circumstances where, from the author's apparent point of view, Adam and Eve were made a *de facto* married couple in an arrangement where Adam exercised hegemony. While it might be argued that the Bible as a whole says much about the inferior role of women in public life, the passage under reference definitely does not, and it would not be too radical to assert that the proper correctives to Biblical misogyny have come not from the Church but from a series of nineteenth-century Married Women's Property Acts, female suffrage legislation, and the developing framework of social security and fair pay.

There are eight apparently clear references to homosexuality. All of these, for a variety of reasons, are of doubtful instructive use; this is a subject which we will explore fully in Section 4.3 (p. 184). It only remains here to note the exiguous representation of the issue. There are no references whatsoever to lesbianism or bisexual practice.

499 of our 900 references comment on power and wealth, their proper use, and the desirability of sacrificing them. Relevant P citations account for 352 out of a total of 640 relevant citations. Even our humble benchmark subject of procedural justice and mercy has a higher score of relevant citations than sex and gender. Or, to put it another way, if we accept that a lack of procedural justice and mercy often goes hand in hand with poverty and political weakness, these two allied topics account for more than 60% of total citations, and 640 (approximately 70%) of citations relevant to sex and gender citations fall below one third.

It is shocking that the Church, despite this clear and conspicuous evidence, should largely still be associated in the general mind with sexual authoritarianism rather than socio-economic radicalism.

PART TWO: SCRIPTURE, TRADITION, REASON & EXPERIENCE

In the second part of this investigation, I will submit the Scriptural references of Part One to examination in Chapter 4, testing them against the traditional criteria of the Church of England by asking what do they say in themselves, how have they been understood in Church history, how can reason be applied to them, and what does our experience tell us about what they mean now? The discussion of P references will be very brief because I believe that what I say is not particularly controversial and does not require close argumentation; the section on S references and, within that, those which apparently refer to contemporary homosexuality, will be much lengthier.

In Chapter 5 I will present a broader context within which to judge the Scriptural evidence.

4.   KEY PASSAGES ANALYSED

In this chapter I will subject our P and S references, particularly those in the latter category apparently referring to homosexuality, to close scrutiny without unduly repeating the material in Part One.

4.1.   'P' TEXTS

4.1.1.   Scripture

There is no doubt of the commitment of the Bible to caring for the poor. The Pentateuch is unequivocal and its requirements permeate the whole library of the Hebrew texts.

The first substantive reference to the distribution of resources occurs in Exodus 16 where everybody, regardless of rank or status, receives an identical share of the divine bounty of manna in the wilderness. Subsequently, Exodus 22.1–29 presents a discussion of economic justice which is far more liberal than anything we would contemplate, followed by miscellaneous comments in Chapter 23. Leviticus 19.9–20 expands general ideas to require provision for gleaners, a kind of land tax. This culminates in Leviticus 19.19, with the first statement of the golden rule that Jews must love their neighbour as themselves. Leviticus 25.13–17 declares the Jubilee which is unimaginably generous by today's standards, as is the provision on the remission of debt every seven years in Deuteronomy 15.1–6. Thereafter references to the care of the poor and weak are liberally distributed, notably in the Prophets and egregiously in Isaiah. The great wealth of rulers is commented upon without apparent condemnation, and even with a hint of admiration when it refers to Assyrians and Persians, notably in the Book of Esther, but the only really wealthy ruler of the Chosen People, Solomon, comes to a sticky end (cf. 1 Kings 11.1).

That tradition is carried on even more intensely by Jesus, who makes socioeconomic justice a central plank of his teaching, notably in the Gospel of Luke (specifically the Sermon on the Plain, 6.17–38). As the letters proceed chronologically towards concerns ever more distant from those voiced by Jesus—the nature of 'church', the definition of doctrinal and ethical orthodoxy—they nonetheless retain a deep concern for the poor combined with a sense, in the face of martyrdom, that to be a Christian means that we must endure privation and even suffering. This is particularly apparent in James. I have chosen to subsume the latter category of references under P because it is a crucial Christian—as opposed to Jewish—perception that socio-economic justice demands sacrifice not only of income and wealth, but also of power and place. As history amply demonstrates, these assets are rarely separate: it is unusual to find riches without power and, in spite of constitutional theories of many sorts, it is also unusual to find power without wealth.

Of the 399 P references, I have judged 352 to be relevant to our times. By this I mean that they bear a message with a clear potential impact upon our daily circumstances, despite the difference in context. We must ask how far Old Testament Law should apply to us—and that is a critical question when we come to analyse S references—but the issue is put beyond doubt by the teaching of Jesus.

It would, I conclude, be difficult to argue that the Scriptures are not concerned with socio-economic justice. To be fair, it is of a philanthropic sort, but I do not think it is unwarranted to conclude that the way that such justice is enacted should be understood within its broader socio-economic context. Thus, in our own times, we might propose that philanthropy is not enough and that taxation has a part to play in assisting the poor.

4.1.2. Tradition

Overall, despite the Bible's strong and consistent emphasis on socio-economic justice, the Western Christian Church has a very poor record of engagement. There has never been a time in our tradition when there have not been systems of one sort or another for assisting the poor, from the Deacons in Acts to the Deacons of third-century Rome, from the early simple monasteries to the grand monastic institutions of the high Middle ages, from the religious foundations of the Reformation to the urban missions of the industrial revolution. However, at no time have these efforts been anything like equal to the tendency of the Western Church to associate itself with temporal power and wealth. Indeed, the very salience and exception of the noble efforts that have been made only throw the hinterland of hierarchical Christian indifference into even darker relief. Some people argue that the rot set in with the establishment of the Christian Church in the reign of the Emperor Constantine (b. 272, r. 306–337), and there is some justice in this. Some people argue that it was essential for the Western Church to ally with the forces of stability during the so-called 'dark ages' which, again, is a reasonable proposition. Nevertheless, whatever the underlying causes for the Church's association with power and wealth, it is difficult to argue that this has not been an ever-present reality. It is, perhaps, too easy to rail against the trappings of power and wealth—the art and the vestments, the pomp and the palaces—but a much more serious truth underlies the outward appearance. From the time of Charlemagne (crowned as first Holy Roman Emperor by Pope Leo III on Christmas Day 800 CE) the Western Church allied itself ever more closely with temporal power, providing secular politicians with its intellectual and administrative services. At the Reformation, many Churches, including the Church of England, became creatures of the secular state and did its bidding in the field of doctrine. It is therefore hardly surprising that such Churches shared the socio-economic views of their secular masters—we are all, to a great extent, uncritical vessels of the assumptions of our own times. But as the secular world developed more sophisticated and generous socio-economic theories, the Western Church was oblivious. In the case of the Church of England, that failure is graphically illustrated by the rise of Wesleyanism on the one hand, and the Catholic inner-city missions of the nineteenth century on the other. It is no accident that the Church of England has been referred to as "the Tory Party at prayer".[11] The majority of its worshippers say that they vote Conservative, and in spite of such stirring initiatives as *Faith in The City*, that impression is both deeply etched and just.[12] In spite of the heroic efforts of the Church of England to retain its ubiquity, not least in deprived areas, it is not well suited in its structures, worship, and assumptions to reach out to the poor or to represent their cause.

The root of this modern paralysis is the general fear of the Western Church of the economic theory of Karl Marx and its implementation in a number of countries, notably Russia. There is no doubt that the atheistic stance of Marx—the son of a Rabbi—threatened Christian principles. However, the most intelligent response would have been to accept those aspects of his economic proposals which were congruent with Scripture while rejecting his atheism, and also by making a proper distinction between Marxist theories and their revisionist manifestations in Western Europe. Instead of this, led by the Roman Catholic Church and the United States of America, Western Christianity largely chose to lump all Marxist and post-Marxist political movements into one 'sin bin'. This is not to say that there were not vigorous Christian socialist movements, not least in the United Kingdom where there was a strong link between the nascent Labour Party and Nonconformist churches, but these have always been, and always viewed as, minority lobbyists against ecclesiastical establishment.

In our own day, it is extremely sad to note (and this subject will be dealt with in greater detail in due course) that during the worst economic depression since the 1930s, the Church of England has

---

[11] Even now: see, for example, *Church Times*, 30 January 2014.
[12] *Faith in the City*, Archbishop of Canterbury's Commission (1987).

been obsessed with the twin issues of the validity of women as bishops and of homosexual people as priests. Whilst these issues may be fascinating in themselves, they are, at best, missiologically marginal, and, at worst, completely irrelevant to the poor, whose understandable response has varied from indifference on the one hand to bewilderment and contempt on the other. It is a great pity that the individual efforts of parishes and their clerical and lay leadership in the area of socio-economic justice have been completely overshadowed by this missiological 'car crash'. Clearly, socio-economic justice should never be reduced to a kind of missiological bribe. However, in living the Christian life, we cannot fail to obey the command of Jesus in this respect.

4.1.3. Reason & Experience

For all the economic theories which have been developed since Adam Smith, the fact remains that the one major commodity which poor people lack is money. We might give them better education (though the quality of education for the poor is almost universally less good, even in state systems, than that accorded to the well off), endless advice, sporadic social workers, and copious moral lectures on the evils of alcohol, tobacco, and drugs. Yet the greatest need of the poor is for the employment which will enable them to support a basic standard of living, free of dependency. The Church of England has stoutly refused, on the whole, to take sides in economic debates and has declared itself to be 'above' party politics. It is curious that it should make an exception of economic theory when it feels itself, quite properly, called to comment on almost every other kind of scientific, philosophical, and ethical issue. There is no obvious argument, other than alienating worshippers who disagree with any conclusion, for excluding economic theory from proper Church scrutiny.

As noted earlier, it is understandable that the Church should have gone along with prevailing social and economic arrangements at a time when these were not contested and were of their time (the feudal system being a good example) but what is inexcusable is the refusal to engage when economic theory was contested. A Church that became so vehement in opposition to colonial slavery in the nineteenth century was much less vehement about other colonial and domestic economic arrangements; even though it was obvious almost from the beginning that, for example, the industrial revolution, for all the economic gains it generated, was demeaning and even morally corrupting. One need only read Dickens or Zola to recognise this.– But capitalism, with its fundamental dependency on cheap labour, went largely unscathed, perhaps because the overall condition of the poor steadily improved.

Thus, it is hardly surprising that the conversion of greed from a private vice into a public virtue went largely unremarked. We are now witnessing the inexorable hollowing out of the middle class as the result of rampant plutocracy and feebly regulated global markets and so, perhaps, because the Church of England is largely middle class, we will at last see some reaction.

Yet no matter how grievous the plight of our domestic poor, that is nothing to the ravages suffered by people in developing countries. It is fair to say that the legacy of colonialism, as the bringer of both Western oppression and Western agricultural techniques and disease control, is mixed. However, its legitimacy and operation went largely unremarked by Western Christianity until the 1960s, no doubt because it was justified as the means to carrying the message of Jesus. The post-colonial record is hardly better. This is particularly apparent in countries where Christian Churches have sided with dictators against their own people in the name of anti-Marxism; a charge just about credible in a handful of Latin American countries during the 1970s, but hardly credible anywhere else.

In an era of 24/7 news coverage it is impossible to evade the contrast between wealth and poverty within and between nation states. In a world largely made up of powerful central administrations, it is impossible to evade the issues of the distribution of income, wealth, power, and sacrifice; the last of which is perhaps the most unremarked aspect of liberal democracy and capitalism.

Traditional liberal theory propounded by utilitarians such as Adam Smith, Thomas Hobbes, and Jeremy Bentham, described a socio-economic model in which everybody benefited from freedom, but we know this not to be the case. Redistributive taxation and tax funded public services have provided the major corrective to imbalances in liberal polities. However, in the UK and United States in particular, Christians have been strikingly hostile to redistributive taxation; despite the evidence that party allegiance is indicative of attitudes towards such a system, inequality is bad for the rich as well as for the poor.[13] No one would wish in any way to justify the commission of crime, the maltreatment of women and children, the abuse of alcohol, and drugs or general moral laxity, yet there is an inescapably direct link, noted as far back as the time of Aristotle, between these ills and poverty. There are always individuals or clusters whose behaviour runs counter to this general rule—rich criminals and virtuous paupers—but the general rule holds nonetheless. Moral lectures by the easy living to the severely deprived are no substitute for advocating, and then realising, a more just society.

The one note of optimism is the almost simultaneous recognition of the importance of socio-economic justice in 2013 by Archbishop Justin Welby and Pope Francis with his important caveat that to be effective, the Church must be of the poor as well as for the poor. As I write, Cardinal Vincent Nichols of Westminster has spoken out on behalf of the poor and 26 Bishops of the Church of England, together with 15 other religious leaders, have launched a similar broadside against punitive Government welfare cuts.[14] However, it is still the case that 90 percent of Christians in the United Kingdom think that poor people are responsible for their own poverty; a shocking shift in public opinion towards the agenda of Christian

---

[13] See, for example, Richard Wilkinson and Kate Pickett, *The Spirit Level: Why Equality Is Better for Everyone* (Penguin, 2010).

[14] BBC Radio 4, 15 February 2014; *Daily Mirror*, 20 February 2014.

Fundamentalists such as those who support the Tea Party in the United States.[15]

4.2.   'S' TEXTS

4.2.1.   Scripture

Issues relating to sex and gender (S) are slightly less evenly distributed than references to power and wealth (P), but they are reasonably well distributed throughout the texts. Like P, they are at their least frequent in narrative works. Of the 337 references identified, I have only ruled 138 relevant. Of the 199 ruled out, most refer either to polygamy or are expressions of misogyny, acceptable in their day but not now.

Unlike the P references which are varied in their subject matter and approach, the relevant S references are almost entirely uniform. Of the 138 references ruled relevant, almost all either condemn fornication, adultery, or both or, conversely, praise the virtues of a stable (though often not monogamous) marriage.

The bedrock of Old Testament thinking on marriage, divorce, adultery, and fornication is set out in the Pentateuch. For all the polygamy and sexual double dealing which ranks the survival of the tribal line over strict adherence to a code of sexual ethics, the Pentateuch is fiercely against adultery and fornication. It only permits divorce for men in sharply defined circumstances of matrimonial unfaithfulness by their wives, but all the legislation applies only to the Chosen People, to full members of the Jewish community.

The foundational text on marriage is Genesis 2.24. It is important to consider whether this text, as part of Genesis 1–3, is

---

[15]   *Theos*, 25 February 2014.

fundamentally didactic or aetiological. At a very obvious level, if the human race was to flourish, Adam and Eve were required to procreate and, as they had no choice of partners, they had to settle for each other. It is also necessary to consider whether there is a difference in sexual requirement between the relative condition of the sexes as the result of the Fall, (cf. Genesis 3.16). Then there is the underlying issue of the two, apparently contradictory, accounts of the creation of Adam and Eve, the first simultaneous, the second sequential.

Adultery is numbered among the Commandments; cf. Exodus 20.14 and Deuteronomy 5.18. Thereafter, injunctions against it are spread throughout the Old Testament. On the other hand, somewhat dismissive, or even indulgent, references to prostitution imply at the very least that this was not a serious offence when carried out by a Jewish male and Gentile female, and there is no criticism at all, say, in the Book of Esther, of the sexual practises of Esther herself or her pagan husband, the emperor. Further, as Ross S. Kraemer comments: "Male slave-owners had the legal right to have sex with the persons they owned, both male and female, children and adults" (we will return to this text in Section 4.3 (p. 184).[16] This observation has deep implications for any understanding of the Jewish attitude towards sex because the Law (and this is fundamental to any clear understanding of homosexuality) is not concerned with the act *per se*, but with the act as a social and cultural construct within Judaism. Again, a critical question is how far the detailed injunctions on sex and gender apply today.

However, the limited scope for divorce in the Old Testament is radically shut down by Jesus in the New Testament, who is unequivocal except for the familiar get-out clause of female unfaithfulness; cf. Matthew 5.31–32, Mark 10.2–13, and Luke 18.18. These injunctions can only be avoided by an appeal to considering them within a broader framework because, standing alone, they are irrefutable.

---

[16]   Levin *et al.*, op. cit., p. 538.

Although there is nothing in the Letters which goes against the teaching of Jesus on marriage, it is important to mention Saint Paul's agonising in 1 Corinthians 7 where, in the face of imminent eschatological closure, he is, to say the least, sceptical about marriage. He only supports it for the avoidance of fornication; a special case which, we will see, was extrapolated to the detriment of marriage as a pillar of Christian life.

4.2.2. Tradition

Throughout most of its history, the Western Church has been as guilty of sexual obsession as it has been innocent of economic curiosity, but that obsession has varied in intensity. From the outset, as early as the later Letters, we see an increasing tendency towards misogyny, based perhaps on a self-interested reading of Paul's specific injunctions of sex and marriage, while ignoring the wider context of 'love', and the realities of marriage and female church leadership as depicted in Romans 16. By the time of the later letters, the fact that it was women who first found the empty tomb and were instructed by Jesus to tell the good news as the first Disciples of the Resurrection, had been forgotten. Along with this new misogyny there went an abhorrence of sexual activity in itself. This had started, as we have already noted, with Saint Paul, but as the prospect of the Eschaton receded, the down-grading of marriage below (particularly clerical) celibacy was not reversed, and it received a massive impetus with the growth of a celibate priesthood—not envisaged by Jesus—which set itself apart as a condition of ritual purity. Not for the last time (e.g. Martin Luther on his personal sin), the emotional turmoil of one person, in this case Saint Augustine (354–430), had a profound and lasting influence on events. His own sexual misdemeanours led him to be excoriating about the sexual act itself, even within the context of marriage, and it is therefore no surprise that Pope Gelasius I (r. 492–496) converted the pagan fertility Festival of Lupercalia into a celebration of chastity. Ironically, this evolved into today's

Feast of Saint Valentine which celebrates romantic and erotic love. As a salutary footnote, Saint Bernard of Clairveaux (1090–1153) managed to deliver 86 sermons of his incomplete commentary on the *Song of Songs* without its ever apparently occurring to him that the poem had any erotic content!

With the development of the feudal system and the beginnings of nation-state monarchies, marriage became necessary to regulate property and inheritance. The Church obliged, frequently finding get-out clauses when secular policy required them, although notably not in the case of King Henry VIII of England, whose divorce case arose precisely at the time when the relatively lax sexual conduct of the Middle Ages was abruptly brought to a halt by the coincidence of three factors. First, although the Protestant reformers emphasised that salvation could only be gained through faith in Christ and not by "works"; paradoxically, they could not resist the temptation to regulate the lives of their flocks in general and their sexual conduct in particular, not least because of their civic power in quasi-theocratic states . This propensity to exercise power over sexual conduct was greatly exacerbated by the second factor: the arrival in Europe of new sexually transmitted diseases from the Americas. Finally, the emergence of a middle class with its own property interests saw an increased percolation of marriage down from the nobility to the bourgeoisie.

The change in the cultural climate can be illustrated by quotations from the Marriage Service. In the York Manual the bride is called upon to be: "bonare and buxum in bedde and at the borde".[17] On the other hand, the *Book of Common Prayer*, after noting that the primary purpose of marriage is for the procreation of children, continues, echoing 1 Corinthians 7, that it is

> Not by any to be enterprised, nor taken in hand . . . to
> satisfy men's carnal lusts and appetites, like brute beasts
> that have no understanding . . . it was ordained as a remedy

---

[17]   Brian Cummings (ed.), *The Book of Common Prayer* (Oxford University Press, 2011), p. 713.

against sin, and to avoid fornication; that such persons as
have not the gift of contingency might marry, and keep
themselves undefiled members of Christ's body.

At least the BCP concedes, on behalf of Saint Paul, that marriage
is honourable!

As prosperity steadily percolated downwards marriage became
ever more necessary for good order and social control, such that
it was legally regularised in Lord Hardwick's Marriage Act of 1753
and, consequently, universal by the mid-nineteenth century. But the
tide in its favour began to turn with the first of a series of Married
Women's Property Acts in 1870, which removed the first obstacle
to divorce. In the twentieth century, the emancipation of women,
propelled by their roles in the two World Wars and increasing
presence in the work force (in 2014 it reached 14 million), and the
associated expansion of social security provision made divorce ever
more possible. With the Divorce Reform Act (1969), where the
concept of 'no fault' divorce was introduced, it became still easier.

In summary, then, contrary to the protestations of contemporary
clerics, the Western Church was initially deeply hostile to marriage
and ranked it below celibacy until the Reformation. There is a
strong case to be made that it has only accommodated itself to
marriage in deference to secular requirements for the regulation of
property transactions and the sexual conduct of the lower classes.
As an interesting footnote, *Hymns Ancient & Modern New Standard*
contains one specifically marriage hymn out of 533 and *The New
English Hymnal* (1986) contains two out of 500.

Nonetheless, the Church of England has considerably modified
its position on marriage. The purposes of marriage in the current
Common Worship says:

Marriage is a gift of God in creation through which husband
and wife may know the grace of God. It is given that as man
and women grow together in love and trust, they shall
be united with one another in heart, body and mind, as
Christ is united with his bride, the Church. The gift of

marriage brings husband and wife together *in the delight and tenderness of sexual union* and joyful commitment to the end of their lives [my italics].

Marriage: A Teaching Document begins by stating that: "Marriage is a gift of God in creation" supported by a scriptural trajectory towards the monogamous, lifelong commitment of one man and one woman.[18] Acknowledging its own past, the document goes on:

The social and emotional steps by which couples come to enter marriage are often complicated, and some finally think about lifelong commitment only when they are living together. This route of approaching marriage is exposed to uncertainties and tensions and is not to be recommended. But it was not uncommon in earlier periods of history, *and the important thing is simply that the point of commitment should be reached* [my italics].

In a single sentence, the Bishops have swept away any condemnation of what, by the standards of the Bible, would be considered to be blatant fornication. This is excused not on doctrinal but on admirably pragmatic grounds: it's all right as long as things turn out for the best.

When it comes to marriage itself, its existence is justified by natural law and pragmatism as well as Scripture: "The words 'till death us do part' are not a special religious ideal; they describe the form of relationship that God has given to human beings as a natural endowment. Knowing that they both must one day die, the partners offer each other a security and continuity in life".[19] There are differing Christian traditions about the status of marriage as a sacrament but:

---

[18] *Marriage: A Teaching Document* (House of Bishops, 1999).
[19] Ibid.

> The description of Christian marriage as a 'sacrament' is valued because it has its source in the New Testament (the "great mystery" of Eph 5.32) although the term does not have exactly the same sense as when it is applied to the two 'sacraments of the Gospel', Baptism and Eucharist. It means that the pledged relation of husband and wife is a sign of the pledge of love that Christ has for his Church.[20]

We have already noted the dangers of the metaphor.

Considering the issue of divorce and re-marriage, the document says:

> All Christians believe that marriage is indissoluble in the sense that the promises are made unconditionally for life . . . well-known words used for centuries, are decisive for what it means to undertake marriage. Some strands of the Western Church have concluded from this that a divorce decree is ineffective and a subsequent marriage invalid in the eyes of God. The reformers of the Church of England did not believe that this was taught in Scripture, and they did not teach it in the Book of Common Prayer; in this respect they came closer to the understanding of the Eastern Church, which allows for the possibility of the 'death' of a marriage. Yet from the Seventeenth century until the present century English Church law made no allowance for a second marriage in the lifetime of a previous partner; and some Anglican Christians have believed, and still do, that such a marriage is, strictly speaking, impossible. These convictions demand respect, though they are not those of the Church of England as a whole.[21]

It is difficult to know what this means because the founding theologians of the Church of England surely understood the

---

[20]   Ibid.
[21]   Ibid.

teaching of the Old Testament confirmed by Jesus. They were, perhaps, influenced by their foundation history: the Church of England was founded on the ruins of lifelong marriage.

The document continues, "it is unwise, and may also be uncharitable, for those outside the marriage to attempt to say precisely where the fault lies in any case." Given Matthew 7.1 and Romans 2.1, this would seem to be a serious understatement which is subsequently somewhat redeemed: "At deeper levels of responsibility for breakdown, however, the Church is not interested in assigning blame to one partner or the other but in helping people accept responsibility for what they have done."

Addressing the central issue, the document says:

> To marry again after divorce may compound the wrong that one has done . . . It may sometimes be a sign of emotional immaturity, and it may also be imprudent, emotionally and financially. In other circumstances, on the other hand, it may be responsible, prudent and emotionally wise. There is no simple rule for discerning this . . . but the Church has learned to stress the importance of putting a clear distance between a new marriage and the old.[22]

Again, this lacks any doctrinal contours and is admirably pragmatic. The document goes on to say that

> It is for the partners . . . to decide whether to marry. But it is . . . for the Church itself, to decide whether the marriage ought to be witnessed and solemnised in an act of worship . . . The breach of marriage is so serious a matter that entering a second one is not something which anyone can claim as a right. When a Christian in this situation has judged it appropriate to marry again, the Church has been willing to respect that decision and to pray with the couple; but it has not been willing to solemnise the marriage . . .

---

[22]   Ibid.

> a further marriage after divorce is an exceptional act . . . it
> must be approached with great honesty and circumspection
> . . . the Church itself . . . has a part in deciding whether or
> not a marriage in such circumstances should take place in
> the context of church worship.[23]

Here, having conceded the general principle, the document then takes back some of its magnanimity with the get-out clause of the "exceptional act", and then by drawing a distinction between "praying with the couple" and agreeing to "solemnise" the marriage. The first point raises the issue of how exceptional is exceptional; the second point raises profound questions about the Church's theology of prayer. Is a solemnising ceremony in some way more effective than simply praying with the faithful? If marriage is considered to be a sacrament then there might be some justice in the distinction, but on this point the Bishops are, as we have seen, equivocal.

What this whole argument comes down to, then, is the granting or withholding of a public ceremony in church to affirm the new marriage before family, friends, and community. According to the Bishops' own statement, this is not a doctrinal issue at all—and for many Christians it never has been. It is, rather, an assertion of clerical power. It is up to the individual cleric, in consultation with the couple wishing to re-marry, to decide whether they are 'worthy' of a marriage ceremony. I speak from personal experience when I say that such a withholding is immensely hurtful for faithful Christians who rank equally the church where they worship and the home where they live.

---

[23]   Ibid.

4.2.3. Reason & Experience

After securing food, securing the survival of the species is our most powerful, natural, God-given drive (cf. the exceptions to accepted sexual ethics to secure tribal survival in the Book of Genesis), and just as we need to regulate competition for resources, so it is sensible to regulate the competition for mates. We know that if sexual conduct goes unregulated that the tendency will be for males to mate with a succession of women with a progressively widerdisparity in age, leaving children with their natural mothers along the way. While we might object to such self-indulgence, the real point is the emotional effect which such behaviour has on the abandoned women and their children. The Church's emphasis is on the responsibilities of parents towards children, but the adherence to a definition of marriage as a lifelong commitment between one man and one woman as the sole relationship where sexual intercourse should take place has three drawbacks.

First, the definition does not connect scientific developments in contraception with the sexual practises of the young and unmarried. This means that any criticism of such behaviour is, in effect, a condemnation of the act in itself outside marriage, but the important point is to separate the exercise of power from mutual enjoyment. The separation of potential procreation from sexual pleasure through reliable contraception raises a host of issues which have hardly been addressed by Christianity, which has tended to resort to undifferentiated moral outrage in spite of the near universal practice in the Western world of people living together before marriage. To that extent, the pragmatic approach cited above is wise, but it should lead to a much clearer definition of what sexual sin might really be.

Secondly, a great many married couples whose marriages break down delay divorce until their children have left home. While this adheres to the notion of commitment, it is conceivable at least that such children are more damaged by living in a broken marriage than living out of it. However, the thought needs to go further. It is very difficult to find a reasonable justification for opposing re-marriage by couples who have fulfilled their responsibilities to their children in first marriages and are not acting against the wishes of the spouse they wish to divorce. Contested divorces raise serious issues, but the presumption cannot be that just because divorces are not unanimously acceptable to two divorcing couples, a church solemnised re-marriage cannot take place. An even more difficult issue for the Church is the distinction it wishes to make between the wish of a couple to marry who meet long after each of their divorces, as opposed to a couple who fall in love when one or both of them is still married. This leads to a dangerously simple concept of "fault" according to which individual clergy can grant or refuse a solemnisation.

Thirdly, marriage was envisaged at a time when all but a few—and most of them rich—could expect to be sexually active from the age of twelve and die before the age of forty. This casts the concept of "lifelong" into a wholly different context. Our experience shows us that people change over time and that two people may, in spite of their best efforts, grow further apart rather than closer together.

For these three reasons, it is proper for the Church of England to be far broader in its approach to marriage and divorce, and to put much more emphasis on the really important issues in the area of sex and gender, namely:

- The use of sexual power, largely by men over women
- The denial by men of their promises to women who have borne and care for the children they have sired, inside and outside marriage (increasingly the latter)
- The sexualisation of minors and the ubiquity of pornography
- The sexual abuse of children, including trafficking, female genital mutilation, and child pornography
- The 'gender gap'
- Misogyny, a phenomenon still shamefully salient in the Church.

Although there will always be devious and manipulative people and doubtful cases, we are all pretty well experienced at assessing the state of a relationship as permanent and faithful. Our experience also tells us that the traditional bar on sex before marriage and lifelong, monogamous marriage, for whatever combination of reasons (reliable and cheap contraception, the peer defined cost of marriage, longevity), are increasingly difficult to sustain. Unless we adopt an irrationally sweeping conclusion that society as a whole is becoming increasingly wicked, we have to accept that there are explanations for these changes which we must take seriously. In spite of society's obsession with sex, there is much about it, particularly at the macro-cultural level, that we do not understand.

The contrast between the Roman Catholic Church and the Church of England is instructive because what it shows us is that people will make up their own mind about proper sexual conduct, in and outside marriage, and will regard this as a culturally superior but doctrinally subordinate set of issues which does not in any way make their Christian faithfulness less authentic. In general terms, the Church of England follows social trends (although painfully slowly) while Roman Catholics follow the same trends in spite of the Magisterium. This brings us back to where this discussion began: when it comes to food and sex there is a need for rules in order to limit competition, but those rules will always be the absolute minimum required to avoid social breakdown. We need to understand better how far behaviour is determined by deeply ingrained biological characteristics, and how far these can be modified without causing damage by crossing the line from self-control into self-repression.

4.3.   HOMOSEXUALITY

4.3.1.   Scripture

There are eight references which are commonly agreed to refer in some manner or other to the sinfulness of homosexuality, although the last of these is not considered relevant in the so-called Pilling Report to which I will return in due course:[24]

1. Genesis 13.3, 19.1–11
2. Leviticus 18.22
3. Leviticus 20.13
4. Judges 19
5. Romans 1.18–32
6. 1 Corinthians 6.9–11
7. 1 Timothy 1.8–10
8. Jude 7.

To begin with, I think it is fair to say that none of the authors had in mind the kind of homosexual relationships at issue today. I accept that Keith Sinclair, the Bishop of Birkenhead, in his Minority Report to the Pilling Report (paragraph 4) has produced evidence that stable homosexual relationships flourished in the pagan world at the time when the New Testament was being written, but he shows no evidence that Saint Paul or the other New Testament writers knew any of these sources or the phenomenon they describe. What is not at issue is the invalidity of homosexual acts which involve violence, coercion, prostitution, promiscuity, or relations with minors.

With reference to the individual citations noted above:

- Genesis 13.3 and 19.1–11 (1) concerns gang rape which rules

---

[24]   *The House of Bishops Working Group on Human Sexuality* (Church House Publishing, November 2013).

it out of contention, and it may in any case be concerned with the hospitality due to angels which must take precedence over the dreadful treatment of the women involved.

- Leviticus 18.22 (2) and Leviticus 20.13 (3) are unequivocal but, if Kraemer's point in Levin *et al* is accepted, that homosexuality between masters and slaves was acceptable in Jewish Law, then it is not the act in itself that is in question but the class of persons involved in it
- Judges 19 (4) suffers the same disadvantages of 1.
- Romans 1.18–32 (5) may well, if we accept the interpretation of Douglas A. Campbell, be speech-in-character rather than Saint Paul's utterance in the first person. The logic in the passage is that idolatrous people are abandoned by God due to the performance of unnatural acts. This is a reversal of Paul's overall theology in Romans and might well, therefore, be speech in the mouth of the opponent that Paul has characterised.
- 1 Corinthians 6.9–11 (6) and 1 Timothy 1.8–10 (7) could not be clearer in themselves
- Jude 7 (8) may refer to angels.

With reference to the general point that what the texts condemn bears no relationship to our contemporary issue, all eight references are relatively weak. Further: 1, 4 and 8 possess additional weaknesses; 2 and 3, on the basis of Kraemer's evidence, do not condemn the act in itself, and if Campbell's argument is accepted, 5 is suspect.

The question then arises of the methodology by which we decide which Biblical ethical standpoints must be taken at face value and which are open to organic interpretation. We have naturally dispensed with all matters concerning Temple worship and sacrifice, together with dietary and clothing laws, and we have accepted, in the case of marriage, that it has evolved away from polygamy and towards monogamy. We have also accepted a development from Law to love between the Two Testaments but, even then, we have had to adjust our ethical stance away from slavery, genocide, and judicial murder (except for a few countries and certain states in the USA). Is there something in the nature of homosexuality which makes it so repugnant that it is in the same ethical category as murder (although even that act is surrounded by a thicket of caveats)? I will argue in Section 4.4 (p. 191), and in a broader context in Chapter 5 (p. 201), that an organic approach to ethics must be all embracing rather than reflecting irrational prejudice.

4.3.2.   Tradition

Let us assume, for the purposes of brevity, that the Western Christian Churches have been strongly opposed to any form of male homosexuality from the death of Christ up until almost the present day, and that the issue of female homosexuality has hardly been considered at all. On that basis, we should begin our discussion with two critical legislative instruments.

The Pilling Report (paragraph 102) quotes the Higton Motion passed by the Church of England General Synod in 1987:

> This Synod affirms that the Biblical and traditional teaching on chastity and fidelity in personal relationships is a response to, and expression of, God's love for each one of us, and in particular affirms:
>
> (1) that sexual intercourse is an act of total commitment which belongs properly within a permanent married relationship;
>
> (2) that fornication and adultery are sins against this ideal, and are to be met by a call to repentance and the exercise of compassion;
>
> (3) that homosexual genital acts also fall short of this ideal, and are likewise to be met with a call to repentance and the exercise of compassion;

(4) that all Christians are called to be exemplary in all spheres of morality, and that holiness of life is particularly required of Christian leaders.

The Report goes on (paragraph 106) to refer to Resolution I.10 of the 1998 Lambeth Conference, which I quote in part:

b. In view of the teaching of Scripture, [this Conference] upholds faithfulness in marriage between a man and a woman in lifelong union, and believes that abstinence is right for those who are not called to marriage;

c. Recognises that there are among us persons who experience themselves as having a homosexual orientation . . . seeking the pastoral care, moral direction of the Church . . ., we commit ourselves to listen . . . we assure them that they are loved by God . . . are full members of the body of Christ . . .

d. While rejecting homosexual practice as incompatible with Scripture, calls on all our people to minister pastorally and sensitively to all . . .

e. Cannot advise the legitimising or blessing of same sex unions nor ordaining those involved in same gender unions.

For completeness, it should be noted that this traditional teaching was strongly upheld in *Issues in Human Sexuality* (1991), in *Some Issues in Human Sexuality* (2003), and in House of Bishops Guidance published in February 2014 following the publication of the Pilling Report in November 2013.[25]

Pilling states the problem it faced as follows in Paragraph 58:

The problem we are unable, collectively, to solve is between the belief that God's purposes revealed in Scripture are eternal, unchanging and consistent, and the plain fact that

---

25   House of Bishops (1991); Church House Publishing (2003) respectively.

> faithful, prayerful Christians who aspire for their lives to be
> governed by Scripture, do not agree about the implications
> of the scriptural texts for same sex relationships. To point
> to the fact of disagreement within the Church is one thing,
> but to validate differing views or to endorse the idea that
> the Church's understanding of the meaning of Scripture
> might change, seems, to some in the Church and on
> our Working Group, to be tantamount to denying that
> Scripture is authoritative to the Church and to opens the
> door to relativistic readings of all Scriptures."

The final caveat and the cause of disagreement are set out fully
in the Bishop of Birkenhead's Minority Report but the rest of the
Working Group was unanimous.

The Report upholds the traditional teaching of the Church of
England as set out above, but it recognises that other views should
be expressed as part of the discernment process (Paragraph 350),
i.e., the matter is not so closed as other paragraphs would suggest,
and it understands the problem which that teaching presents
(Paragraph 144):

> The Church's vocation is to bring the whole people into the
> presence of that loving God, and it cannot do so if it is only
> willing to acknowledge the aspects of the person and their
> relationships which are already acceptable. If the Church is
> to live up to its vocation, it must find ways to acknowledge
> and address effectively the messiness of the relationships
> through which people express their sexual natures . . .

As to the 'cause' of the phenomenon of homosexuality, the Working
Group concludes that the science is inconclusive, that there is no
consensus on the major issues and that change is therefore not
justified, but that a pastoral approach which respects homosexuals
and combats homophobia is greatly to be desired. It also recognises
that many homosexuals will want to take part in Civil Partnerships
and in 'gay' marriage, but the depth of its confusion is revealed

in Paragraph 373 when it says: "it is entirely legitimate for the Church to require higher standards of conduct from its clergy than for the laity", and that, therefore, 'gay' clergy cannot be involved in non-celibate homosexual relationships. There are two forces in play here: first, homosexuality is seen as a lower standard of behaviour than that which the Church requires, but secondly, and pragmatically, the Church, for the laity at least, has to recognise homosexuality as a fact of Church life which must be dealt with.

As with divorce and re-marriage, the issue is the form of Church prayer that can be accorded to lay homosexual relationships.

4.3.3.   Reason & Experience

There is still a fascinating debate about the nature of homosexual desire which, put somewhat over-simply, revolves around the question of whether it is a natural, and therefore God-given, phenomenon or the exercise of a preference which the Bible condemns. On this point Pilling sticks to the evidence offered by medical psychology which, it says, is inconclusive. In view of well documented cases of complex sexuality resulting from a mis-match of genitalia appropriate to one's sex and hormones appropriate to the other while the putative person is still in the foetus, and manifestations of 'gay' behaviour in young boys all of whose parental and cultural influences are hostile (the well documented case of Boy George comes to mind), this is a curiously reticent conclusion, but there is a wider horizon to consider.

There is, I believe, a strong possibility that homosexual desire is a collectively regulated phenomenon such as that which alters the birth rate gender ratio in favour of men after major wars and, nearer to the situation we are discussing, the fall in natural female fertility—quite distinct from the use of contraception—both as female education levels rise and as the species in a given location is less likely to be endangered. In other words, there is evidence to suggest that increased and localised (as opposed to global) prosperity increases not only the mean time between births but also the number of women incapable of conceiving by natural means. Although homosexual desire is not restricted to the prosperous and welleducated (two phenomena which are themselves inter-linked), it is certainly much more salient in these population groups; it would not be at all surprising if the phenomenon of homosexuality directly relates to localised increases in prosperity and the declining drive for species survival. If that is so, if this is a 'Gaia-like self-regulating demographic phenomenon, then, over time, its relevance will spread beyond post-industrial countries to the prosperous segments of poorer countries which have, paradoxically urged on and financed by Evangelical Churches in the United States, conflated homosexuality with imperial and post-imperial decadence.[26]

There have been, I believe, three major complicating factors in coming to grips with the concept of stable, faithful, homosexual relationships:

- Many homosexuals are not only reticent about their desires but some, not least clergy (cf. the case of Cardinal Keith O'Brien), actually deny the validity of the desire they experience
- Out of ignorance or prejudice, homosexuality is frequently conflated with child abuse
- It cannot be denied that some homosexual males express their homosexual desire in appalling promiscuity[27]. But just as we do not conflate faithful, heterosexual marriage with wanton heterosexual promiscuity just because the sex act is involved, so we should be more forensic in examining the nature of homosexual desire.

There is a strong opinion in some Church quarters that, while homosexuality cannot be denied—which is not quite the same thing as, although very close to, saying that it is natural in creation—

---

[26]   cf. James Lovelock's Gaia hypothesis.
[27]   cf. Randy Shilts, *And the Band Played On* (Saint Martin Press, 1987).

desire should not be expressed in sexual acts but should be resisted or, to use contemporary psychological terminology, suppressed. Apart from the problem of defining celibacy, it is important to understand the psychological effect of unexpressed desire. One further question of some importance to the Church is why such a high proportion of clergy are homosexual compared with all other occupational/vocational groups other than those involved in the arts? Experience surely tells us that this is no coincidence.

On the whole, the debate about the validity of the expression of homosexual desire is very similar to that concerning the validation of the rightness of ordaining women as priests, or the broader political controversy about immigration and a multi-racial society: the more we see of a phenomenon and, therefore, the more familiar we are with it, the less prejudiced we are likely to be and, therefore, the less hostile.

4.4. SYNTHESIS

One major issue remains to be discussed in this Chapter: if the Western Churches have been so careless of the socio-economic responsibilities which the teaching of Jesus requires, and if the Church of England and some other non-Catholic Churches have abandoned, in all but name, any condemnation of fornication as it manifests itself in couples coming to the marriage altar accompanied by their children, and any condemnation of Biblically defined adultery through permitted re-marriage after divorce, why are they so tenacious in their much less Biblically justified hostility to homosexuality?

Without wishing to labour the point, the Biblical evidence for the Christian obligation to care for the weak and the poor is overwhelming, and the teaching of Jesus on marriage could not be clearer. Yet the Church of England and other Christian churches have largely ignored the former, apparently without much of a bad conscience, until recent times, and have found what they believe to be Biblically justified ways of coming to terms with sexual intercourse outside marriage and with re-marriage after divorce. So why not the same accommodation for homosexuality?

To answer the question we need to deal with three issues:

- The relationship between broad Biblical concepts and individual pericopes
- The relationship between doctrine and pastoral care
- The moral purpose of Christianity.

4.4.1.   Concepts and Pericopes

The proposal to liberalise provision for homosexual people in the Pilling Report was set out in David Runcorn's submission which, though poorly argued, relies upon the principle that broad themes subsume awkward anomalies. Put simply, the argument is based on the somewhat simplistic slogan: "What would Jesus do?" But, as a strategy, this is just not good enough. As we know from the Gospels, the great virtue of Jesus is not what he did but what he failed to do, notably his failure to judge people or society on specific issues. As Jesus left slavery precisely where he found it, it is not any specific teaching—or even a broad swathe of teaching—that can be invoked to support nineteenth-century reform. What matters is not what Jesus would have done but what we should do in the light of all we know from the Bible in general and the teaching of Jesus in particular. This involves, as we have noticed, an understandable tendency to unload a great deal of Old Testament legal baggage, but this has not entirely solved the problem because of the agonised and frequently contradictory writing of Saint Paul, who spent his itinerant life forging Christianity from scratch, before the Gospels were written. It is undeniable that Paul's central tenet is love (cf. 1 Corinthians 13) but, unlike Jesus, he is not so strict, in spite of Romans 2.1 (how could he be as a fallible human being?), in refusing to judge the conduct of others. Overall, however, it would be perverse to rank any such lapses by Paul higher than his general tenet. It would also be blasphemous to rank Paul's pronouncements on any issue above those of Jesus. To say that the Bible is to be read as a whole is not the same as to say is that everything it has to say is equally valid.

Even though the four Gospels are very different, it is remarkable how consistently Jesus' moral stance comes across. Without any inconsistency, he proclaims the Kingdom of God on earth—a large part of which involves socio-economic justice—and refrains from judgment. On that basis, it does not seem unreasonable to derive a set of ethics for the Christian (as opposed to Christian ethics) based on the New Testament, except where there is an egregious case for ranking the Old over the New. In the case of our three sets of issues, there seems to be no good reason to rank anything in the Old Testament over what is expressed in the New. On this basis, it is justifiable to subject our moral conduct to New Testament teaching and, within that, to give Jesus priority over Paul. On the slavery issue, for example, we are entitled to say not that Jesus should have anticipated ethical changes outside his chronological time, but that we should understand what he said and did not say as a template against which to judge our contemporary issues. On this basis, Christians came to understand slavery as an ill within the framework of Christ's teaching on the dignity of human beings, that all people are made in God's image, and, on that basis, for example, it is fundamentally un-Christian for North American Christian conservatives to neglect the poor and the weak because they believe that there is something fundamentally obnoxious in the power of the federal state. If they are not prepared to live simply, giving all they have to the poor, then the only other available option to assist the poor is compulsory taxation. Likewise, on the issue of pre-marital sexual intercourse and post-divorce re-marriage, while the individual citations are all contrary to contemporary practice, the fundamental question remains: what do we understand by love and how do we live out that understanding in our time? Whatever the answer might be, it cannot be that how we live out love is defined for us by a self-perpetuating religious hierarchy. If these principles apply to the broad areas of economics and sexual conduct, then they apply no less to the special case of homosexuality.

Finally, to end this section on a somewhat sour note, there is more than a whiff of self-interest—always a phenomenon of which we should be deeply suspicious—on the part of Christians who, for example, oppose the redistribution of income and wealth, but support re-marriage after divorce; who oppose abortion but support capital punishment, and who, in summary, support unlimited economic liberalism while opposing social liberalism.

4.4.2.   Doctrine and Pastoral Care

As to the relationship between doctrine and pastoral care, recent Church of England documents imply—more by accident than design, I think—that pastoral care is a second best option to doctrinal consistency which manifests itself, because the Church of England is defined by its worship and not by doctrine *per se*, in a discussion of what worship rights can be accorded to what class of people or event. This is why the debate about re-marriage after divorce and the nature of homosexual commitment have revolved around liturgical solemnisation and not around doctrinal consistency. Related to this is intense debate about the gender of clergy and their own sexual conduct, as the ecology of worship is fundamental to the Church of England's self-understanding: to express the idea in an exaggerated form, an eminent theologian may live a scandalous life but a priest must not!

This outward appearance of subordinating the pastoral to the doctrinal is, however, misleading. Jesus, as our 'Good Shepherd' was, fundamentally, pastoral and not doctrinal; indeed, like his contemporaries, his only doctrine was to recognise the God of all things. Jesus also recognised both the validity, and the limits, of the Law. Some maintain that Jesus replaced the Law with love, but it might be better to say that he informed ethics with love, justice, and mercy, and, if necessary (and contrary to three centuries of liberal thinkers such as Hobbes, Bentham, John Stuart Mill, and

John Rawls, among others), sacrifice[28]. On this basis, the pastoral is much more important in ethics than the doctrinal which is, in any case, our helpless wrestling with language about God's intentions for us.

In spite of the obvious problems which Pilling set out in Paragraph 58 of the Report which has tended to generate turgid, sometimes incomprehensible, and often contradictory prose, there is no doubt that the Church of England places much greater value on its pastoral heart than on its doctrinal brain, but it needs to take two definite steps to clarify that priority:

- It must say what it knows of itself much more clearly by ranking pastoral considerations above doctrinal consistency (which seems, to my mind, to be a self-evident proposition) and, incidentally, missiological effectiveness over doctrinal elegance.
- It must make it simpler to speak of itself by abandoning the recent tendency to believe that a national, as opposed to a sectarian, Church provides a home for everyone who calls him- or herself Christian.

On this second point, the Elizabethan Settlement was clear about the exclusion of sects—whether Puritan or Catholic—which did not accept its broad Church approach. That approach has been seriously undermined by fundamentalist evangelical entryism not dissimilar to the entryism of the Militant Tendency into the Labour Party in the 1980s which engendered the birth of the Social Democratic Party and then reform under the guise of New Labour. The paradox of this situation is that both traditional Catholics and fundamentalist evangelicals, in opposing the ordination of women as priests, have loudly asserted their integrity as "loyal Anglicans" while, at the same time, respectively invoking their interpretation of catholicity and the authority of Scripture to demonstrate that

---

[28] cf. Paul Khan, *Putting Liberalism in Its Place* (Princeton University Press, 2008).

the majority of members of the Church of England, positioned 'between' these two extreme wings, are not faithful Anglicans.

4.4.3.   The Moral Purpose of Christianity

One of the great dangers posed by fundamentalism forms the core of our third issue: the moral purpose of Christianity, an issue which has been seriously complicated by hierarchical clerical power. If, as we noted, the two major natural drives in human existence are nutrition and procreation, the regulation of the latter by clerical power has been far more obvious than the much more vital regulation of the former. As I write, the Church of England and other Christian leaders are fulminating about poverty, malnutrition, and the regrettable necessity for food banks, and I suspect, perhaps a little ungraciously, that the rarity of such outbursts accounts to some degree for the mass media coverage. Pronouncements on sexual matters, on the other hand, are so frequent that even a sex-obsessed media gives little space to them. The exercise of power in sexual matters for the imposition and maintenance of orthodoxy, the preservation of good order, or for any other reason, flouts our Christian obligations in three ways:

- The exercise of power in general is alien to the teaching of Jesus
- Jesus was particularly suspicious of the clerical exercise of power and took care to leave behind him a totally non-clerical inheritance.[29]
- Critically, an ethical code based on visible outcomes is shallow and open to manipulation, dissembling, and corruption.

What mattered to Jesus, and what should matter to all Christians, are, contrary to the three issues noted above:

---

[29]   Gary Wills, *Why Priests? A Failed Tradition* (Penguin, 2013).

- The exercise of our free will for the common good
- That the above is explored without the need for, or any attention to, hierarchical, clerical pressure
- Being honest with ourselves in our motivation.

Only God knows why we do what we do, better than any psychologist and certainly better than any moralist more intent on preaching than on listening or watching. Only God knows what hand we were dealt and how well we are playing it.; We are always subject to the reality that we were created imperfect as a necessary precondition for exercising free will and, therefore, being enabled to choose freely to love God and our neighbour in the widest sense. To rail against imperfect humanity is to rail against our God-given condition; in that sense, our wrong decisions are a necessary collateral down-side of our freedom to love.

In summary, then, the reason why homosexuality has found itself in an anomalous situation in the context of the use of Scripture to determine right human behaviour is that:

- Firstly, the broad purpose of God for man set out in the Bible has been subjugated to pericopic nit-picking
- Secondly, the doctrinaire has too frequently been ranked above the pastoral
- Thirdly, there has been a Christian obsession with exercising hierarchical clerical (mostly celibate) power over the sexual conduct of, in hierarchical terms at least, inferiors
- Finally, and fatally, moral debate has focused on outcome rather than motive.

One can only wish that the Church of England will find more courage to follow its instincts after a period when it has been caught up with Roman Catholic dogmatic obsession and Evangelical literalism; the former largely ignoring the Bible, the latter treating it like a chemistry textbook. As the Pilling Report wisely remarks (Paragraph 59),

> The meaning and implications of Scripture are, of course,
> filtered through the fallible and sinful minds of human
> beings. But the safeguard here has always been the Church.
> Without claiming infallibility for the Church on earth, the
> Church's vocation is to discern the will of God for the world
> and to do so it must, as far as is possible, come to a shared
> mind about how to apply the Scriptures in each generation.

But it depends whom we are sharing with.

The Church of England has paid as high a price for its
comprehensiveness as Roman Catholicism has paid for its
narrowness. The conventional way that this is put (Pilling,
Paragraph 446) is that the Church's stance on homosexuality has
presented a missiological challenge, particularly among the young.
I would argue that the Church's obsession with marginal sexual
and gender issues might well have damaged the Church's mission
but I can endure that, even as a lover of the Church of England,
as long as it does not damage Christ's mission. Of course, as that
mission is in the power of the Holy Spirit, it cannot be damaged.
A structured Church has much to offer a confused world but the
price of keeping it, in terms of its obscuring of rather than clarifying
the good news of Jesus Christ, may just be too high.

Yet the events of recent months bring us hope that the emphasis
might be shifting in Western Christianity; not only because of the
recent ecclesiastical interest in poverty, but because of answers
Pope Francis gave in his interview of August 2013::

> A person once asked me, in a provocative manner, if
> I approved of homosexuality. I replied with another
> question: "Tell me: when God looks at a gay person, does
> he endorse the existence of this person with love, or reject
> and condemn this person?" We must always consider
> the person . . . In life, God accompanies persons, and we
> must accompany them, starting from their situation . . .
> The dogmatic and moral teachings of the church are not
> all equivalent. The church's pastoral ministry cannot be

obsessed with the transmission of a disjointed multitude of doctrines to be imposed insistently. Proclamation in a missionary style focuses on the essentials, on the necessary things: . . . we have to find a new balance. Otherwise even the moral edifice of the church is likely to fall like a house of cards, losing the freshness and fragrance of the Gospel. The proposal of the Gospel must be more simple, profound, and radiant. It is from this proposition that the moral consequences then flow.[30]

Amen.

---

[30] Antonio Spadaro, SJ, *A Big Heart Open to God: A Conversation with Pope Francis* (HarperOne, 2013).

5.   HANDING BACK THE SILVER

At no point in the Gospels does Jesus condemn anyone for individual wrong-doing and, with an aching irony that should trouble sexual moralists, on the one occasion when he might have been most expected to do so (John 8.1–11, although probably a fragment of Luke) where a woman is said to have been caught in the very act of adultery (8.3), Jesus says when he sees that the would-be stone-throwers have all departed: "Has no one condemned you . . . Neither do I condemn you." (John 8.10–11). Perhaps, on a point of procedural justice, Jesus wondered what had happened to the man but, in view of his conduct and pronouncements as a whole, it is more likely that he was simply following his usual practice when confronted by behaviour which went against the Law.

The claim of the Church of England, much more modest than that of the Church of Rome, to pronounce on moral matters is summed up in Paragraph 59 of the Pilling Report:

> The meaning and implications of Scripture are, of course, filtered through the fallible and sinful minds of human beings. But the safeguard here has always been the Church. Without claiming infallibility for the Church on earth, the Church's vocation is to discern the will of God for the world and to do so it must, as far as is possible, come to a shared mind about how to apply the Scriptures in each generation.

I infer from the context that the Church is referring to the moral matter of homosexuality rather than making a claim about doctrine.

From ancient times, the Western Church has claimed authority over many matters based on Matthew 16.18–19 and 18.18 respectively:

> And I tell you, you are Peter, and on this rock I will build
> my church, and the gates of Hades will not prevail against
> it. I will give you the keys of the kingdom of heaven, and
> whatever you bind on earth will be bound in heaven, and
> whatever you loose on earth will be loosed in heaven…

> Truly I tell you, whatever you bind on earth will be bound
> in heaven, and whatever you loose on earth will be loosed
> in heaven.

The latter is addressed to the followers of Jesus and not just to Peter as is the former. Now, unless Jesus is hopelessly contradictory, there has to be an explanation of how these two quotations fit with Matthew 7.1: "Do not judge so that you may not be judged." It seems to me that, in the first two instances, Jesus is discussing the power to exclude someone from his followers, first giving the power to Peter but later spreading it to his followers as a whole; a power quite different from pronouncing on individual conduct. The distinction is made clearer in 1 Corinthians 5 where Paul denounces a public scandal and urges a primitive form of excommunication from the believing community. I am inclined to accept the Gary Wills thesis that the transformation–based on the clerical power of the 'miracle' of transubstantiation–from public, communal condemnation of major scandal to the private forgiveness of minor infractions which began in Ireland in the fifth century addicted (my word, not Wills') the church's hierarchy to moral power, an addiction from which it has not fully recovered. In spite of the decline in private confession, there is still an abundance of clerical pronouncement on private behaviour.

In John 5 Jesus does not condemn the woman who has had five husbands and is currently living with a sixth man but, rather, is very gentle. Insofar as John can manage it, Jesus is even a touch humorous. Such behaviour fits well with his address to Nicodemus:

> For God so loved the world that he gave his only Son,
> so that everyone who believes in him may not perish but

may have eternal life. Indeed, God did not send the Son
into the world to condemn the world, but in order that the
world might be saved through him. Those who believe in
him are not condemned; but those who do not believe are
condemned already, because they have not believed in the
name of the only Son of God.

This passage raises the legitimate question of whether belief
requires a certain lifestyle in order to be genuine. Perhaps it does,
but that lifestyle in part consists of not condemning others; that is
what Jesus says of his lifestyle and it is he whom we must imitate.
Jesus goes on to say that not only should we not judge others but
that we cannot: "You judge by human standards; I judge no one.
Yet even if I do judge, my judgment is valid; for it is not I alone
who judge, but I and the Father who sent me." This leaves over
the question of whether the Church, unable to judge by God's
standards, should judge by human standards.

In addition to the issues of the connection between lifestyle and
belief, and the difference between divine and human judgment,
there is a third issue raised on numerous occasions by Jesus which
is best summed up in Matthew 15.18. This is repeated in Mark 7.20
and in Luke 6.45 (though in a slightly different form), which clearly
draws a distinction between motive and outcome; a distinction
which modern civil law has heroically attempted to defend but
which has been under ever increasing attack by moralists who wish
to base punishment—which begs yet another of Jesus' questions—
on outcome.

None of the issues raised so far is difficult to settle. With respect
to motive, a Christian is bound to admit that s/he does not know
anything about the relationship between the Creator and creatures
at an individual level and therefore cannot fathom the complex
issue of motive. We do not know the hand which anybody else
has been dealt by God nor how well or badly each is playing it. No
matter how hard we try and no matter how minutely we enquire,
we will never fully understand the motive for any action, even
if the person being interrogated thinks he knows precisely why

he did something. At a fundamental philosophical level, no two people can experience precisely the identical emotion at a precisely identical time in a precisely identical place with precisely identical antecedent life experiences. The case of judging on the basis of motive is hopeless and the case for judging on outcome is unethical. The issue is further complicated by our increasing bewilderment about where 'evil' ends and 'sickness' begins. Is a mass murderer mentally ill or plain evil? As far ahead as we can see, science is not going to solve this problem for us. So much for the judgment of human beings.

Secondly, how far is lifestyle connected with belief? The case on our first point makes the idea of lifestyle being connected with belief pretty hopeless. The Church, whose modest but definitive role is cited above from Pilling (Paragraph 59) has permitted all kinds of lifestyles in its history without asserting that they impair belief. Even now, it would be difficult to find (and I have not found) any pronouncement from the Western Church stating that to earn more than a million dollars a year, or to live on a million dollars of unearned income per year, is immoral. In a strangely paradoxical way to which I will return, the Church has been as outspoken on sexual morality as it has been reticent on social justice.

The third issue is whether the Church should be involved at all in earthly justice when there is the civil power. There was a strong case at the time of Jesus for Jews and early Christians to reject Roman legalism in favour, respectively, of traditional justice based on the Torah and the collective justice of elders. However, now we have a solid system of civil law, largely (though decreasingly) based on Christian values (including perverted Christian values such as severe punishment disproportionately inflicted on the poor), is a Christian, ecclesiastical moralism justified? I can see no harm in this as long as it is voluntary—which the Sacrament of Confession is—and the 'punishments' restorative or constructive. It is somewhat ironic that, in parallel with the Church's continued strictures on homosexual people, it has been a champion of restorative justice.

In summary, then, the case is very weak for the Church, in any guise, individually or collectively, communally or hierarchically, to exercise moral judgment over Christians except where the public scandal of individual behaviour is so great and so clear (the Archbishop of Canterbury living with a harem for the unambiguous purpose of sexual gratification) that a community measure might be considered. Even here, we must be careful of the problem of distinguishing between motive and outcome, and between moral and health issues. It would also be helpful to say at this point that domesticated homosexuality is hardly a great public scandal, which is the justification for Pilling's distinction between acceptable conduct for the laity and the clergy. It is difficult to avoid the conclusion that this is not only difficult territory for the Church, but that it is so difficult for any organisation that such issues are best left to the wildly varying and often contradictory endeavours of civil justice, which at best approximates its processes and outcomes to what is generally held to be acceptable, while protecting minorities whose views vary from the normative. But the task of the state—even according to the most conservative political theorists such as Nozick—is to uphold law and maintain order; not my law, not your law, not God's law, but The Law.

It might, conversely, be argued that the primary purpose of justice is to regulate our two strongest biological drives for the survival of the species and the survival of individual members of it because these pose the greatest dangers to order. As it turns out, this is true, but not in the conventional sense. The greatest threats to good order resulting from our biological drives are poverty and domestic murder, which are closely linked. On the whole, the state in liberal societies attempts to regulate against negative behaviour rather than prescribing correct behaviour, and it makes a vital distinction between private and public behaviour; a subject to which we now turn.

There is no doubt that it is perfectly possible to behave badly in private—a person may become obsessed with legitimately acquired wealth—and that this is a proper cause for moral concern. On the other hand, it is not a proper concern of civil justice, but the greater moral concern arises if the wealth is either ill-gotten or simply excessive in the context of social justice. This is where the crucial fault lies in the Western Church's ethical tradition where it has always favoured the private over the public, the individual over the communal.

All human beings—with the exception of a tiny, merely theoretical minority which can live without reference to any other human being (gathering berries and drinking from a spring)—are social creatures which depend for their survival on other human beings. This is not simply a theoretical or a natural law construct; it is a proposition that arises from observation, sharpened in recent times by our greater violation, and understanding, of pollution and climate change. It is how we behave towards others, then, that has the greatest impact on the society in which we are all, by force of circumstance, obliged to live whether we like it or not. It is this inevitability of our being which drives our moral obligation. From this standpoint, the denial of social obligation based on the necessity of communal living stands at the opposite end of the moral spectrum from a consensual homosexual relationship which is socially less damaging than a heterosexual divorce, or a promiscuous heterosexual relationship which results in the procreation of children for which one or both parties renounce responsibility. Even if such responsibilities are recognised, they cannot be fully honoured where a parent has obligations to children within different, fractured households. Compared with the consensual homosexual relationship which produces no children but which might care for unwanted children, the evils of poverty resulting from injustice are egregious, damaging both the unjust and those who suffer from injustice. From a pragmatic standpoint, therefore, it is proper to rank the social above the individual and not only in the sphere of economic justice. There have been many individuals, for example, who have abandoned their personal ambition to enjoy romantic love in order to maintain family cohesion or who have abandoned personally satisfying careers for social causes. And, of course, millions of people in our liberal democracies have voluntarily given up their lives, or been wounded, in what they have understood to be the defence of shared social values. Our society places a very high priority on individual freedom, particularly in the pursuit of romantic love, but we are still so fundamentally social that we could not imagine living in any other way.

One way of looking at social injustice is to see it within geographically narrow contexts such as districts within a town where people subject to the same laws and the same sales taxes have radically different life chances because of, among other things, the accident of to whom and precisely where they were born, the standard of their physical nutrition, housing, and intellectual and moral education. Such differences are not inevitable because we know they vary within societies; it is an observable fact that there is less economic injustice in Scandinavia than there is in the United States of America. It is also an observable fact that injustice varies within countries according to legislative provision, particularly in respect of the role of the state in redistributing income and wealth. *Pace* Catholic Social Teaching, and increasingly frequent and vehement interventions by the Church of England, the failure of Western Christianity to be an active advocate for social justice 'at home' has been egregious.

Another way of looking at social injustice is to compare conditions across borders; perhaps the most immediately vivid being that between the United States and Mexico. In this matter the Western Christian Churches have been much more emphatic than they have been on justice within single countries. Christian Aid and similar organisations are a tribute to this approach to justice but they paradoxically expose the failure to deal with domestic injustice.

There is no doubt that crime and socially irresponsible behaviour go hand-in-hand with poverty induced by injustice and that, therefore, justice is a better moral corrective than preaching; a perception shared by secular commentators and Jesus—but not by a large number of Christian moralists—who preached the Kingdom on earth as it is in heaven. As I noted in passing in the Introduction (p. 1), opponents of the consecration of women as bishops denounced the social justice argument as inferior to the ecclesiological and representational arguments; neither of which Jesus would have recognised. The struggle for social justice is as essential to Christianity as the Resurrection. The same cannot be said of arbitrary, hierarchically delivered moral strictures on well-motivated private behaviour which some people find offensive.

At the heart of this debate, however, there lies a deep and tragic truth which is that Western Christianity is in thrall to a deeply heretical obsession with personal salvation based on private behaviour, which is at once Pelagian and selfish.

What the doctrines of indulgences and purgatory began, Protestantism, paradoxically, completed. It was but a short step from the lenient and meddlesome transactions of the confessional to a Pelagian economy which set a price on salvation which combined righteous individual conduct and philanthropy. In opposing the schema of indulgences, adopting justification by faith alone, based on *sola scriptura*, Protestantism still could not resist the temptation to use theocratic power to regulate individual, particularly sexual, behaviour. This was not least because it could never solve the problem for which the Papal Magisterium was an unsatisfactory but coherent solution: as the meaning of Scripture is not—and often cannot—be clear, who decides what it means and what that means. At the same time, the very bourgeois nature of the theocratic state ruled out an equal concern with economic behaviour. In parallel with this Protestant obsession with sex and hostility to social justice, the Roman Catholic Church's concerns from the Council of Trent onwards were, at the highest level, fundamentally ecclesiological rather than social and, at the parochial level, sexual rather than social The girl pregnant outside wedlock was more of a disgrace than the peasant who died of starvation.

This betrayal of the social for the personal, the socio-economic for the sexual, culminating with an obsession with harmless, private homosexual behaviour during the worst economic crisis for the very poor for eighty years, is the Western Church's greatest act of treachery against Jesus. It is what casts us as the Judas Church.

The Pilling report draws attention to the possibility that to oppose the sanctioning of homosexual relationships may be missiologically challenging (Paragraph 346) but that is to underestimate the extent of the malaise. Of course it will be more difficult to preach the Gospel to people who see the preachers as either misguided or plain wrong on the issue of homosexuality, but the real problem is that the Church's verdict on homosexuality and related issues is seen by many to be the gospel. Some will recognise the Church's role in development assistance in the poorest countries and will recognise what parishes are doing to alleviate the worst excesses of social injustice in our own country. But few will identify the Church with the teaching of Jesus on the establishment of God's kingdom on earth, and that is primarily because, for the clerical and lay leadership of the Western Church, this tenet which was central to Jesus has been, and still is, marginal compared with the drive to control private behaviour.

Judas handed back the silver and killed himself. We should hand back the silver and try to do better.

Lightning Source UK Ltd.
Milton Keynes UK
UKOW04f0453230914

239022UK00007B/102/P